CULTURAL RESOURCES OF THE ALEUTIAN REGION

Gary C. Stein
Research Historian

Volume I

Anthropology & Historic Preservation
Cooperative Park Studies Unit
University of Alaska, Fairbanks

Occasional Papers No. 6
October 1977

CONTENTS

I. INTRODUCTION: THE ALEUTIAN ENVIRONMENT

There are many problems inherent in attempting to fully assess the cultural resources of an area such as that encompassed in the boundaries of the Aleut Corporation. While there are many things which bind the area together into a unified whole, there are also many differences which must be taken into consideration. Yet both the differences and the unifying aspects are, in large part, caused by the geographic location and environmental effects of the region upon its inhabitants.

The Aleut Corporation consists of the Aleutian Islands themselves--a chain of volcanic mountaintops reaching out over 1,100 miles across the northern Pacific; a 200-mile portion of the lower Alaska Peninsula and the island groups (Shumagin, Popov, and Sanak) off the Peninsula's southern coast; and the Pribilof Islands, located in the Bering Sea 300 miles west of the Alaskan mainland and 200 miles north of the Aleutians.

The Aleutian Islands are comprised of five major island groups, from west to east: Near, Rat, Andreanof, Island of the Four Mountains, and Fox. There are well over 100 major islands in the Chain, with innumerable small islands, islets and rocks. The islands are located between $172^\circ 24'$ E (Attu) and $162^\circ 22'$ W (Unimak); the southernmost island (Amchitka) lies at approximately $51^\circ 22'$ N, and the northernmost (Unimak) at $51^\circ 51'$ N. The Pribilof Islands consist of two large islands, St. George and St. Paul, and the smaller Walrus and Otter Islands. The easternmost boundary of the Aleut Corporation lies on the Alaska Peninsula at approximately $160^\circ 00'$ W. Only Amak Island lies off the northern coast of the Peninsula, while the Sanak and Shumagin groups, as well as numerous other islands, lie off the Peninsula's southern coast.

Their position, separating the Bering Sea from the north Pacific, give the Aleutian Islands their most striking characteristic--their climate. Fogs, storms, and high winds are common throughout much of the year. Temperatures, however, though relatively cold are not severely so, and drop below zero only rarely. Most of the Chain is overcast during the year, and measurable precipitation occurs more than two-thirds of the year.[1]

Another characteristic of the Aleutian area is its topography. The islands form the crest of the Aleutian Range extending from the Alaska Peninsula, with volcanic peaks rising on the northern coasts of the islands to as much as 10,000 feet (Shishaldin Volcano on Unimak Island), although elevations are usually less than 5,000 feet. These islands form "one of the world's most active seismic zones."[2] Elevations on the Alaska Peninsula are somewhat higher.

Vegetatively, the Aleutians are characterized by alpine or moist tundra. Due to terrain and climate trees are almost totally absent, except for those transplanted by the Russians onto the Shumagin Islands and Unalaska, and those planted by military servicemen on their Aleutian bases in the 1940s. Plant life in the western Aleutians is typical of

---

[1]
U.S. Fish and Wildlife Service, Aleutian Islands Wilderness Study Report (n.p.: 1973), pp. 6-9; hereafter cited as WSR.

[2]
State of Alaska, Alaska Regional Profiles; Southwest Region, ed. by Lidia L. Selkregg)published by University of Alaska, Arctic Environmental Information and Data Center, n.d.), p. 3; hereafter cited as SW Regional Profile.

that found on the Russian Kamchatka Peninsula, while that of the eastern Islands is similar to that of the Alaska Peninsula, where there is a greater abundance of wet tundra in the marshy areas of the Peninsula's northern coast (and the northern coast of Unimak, in the eastern Aleutians), and high brush (not found on the islands at all) on the southern coast. Fewer plants are found in the central Aleutians than in the eastern or western extremes.[3] Marine vegetation is quite abundant, and an important source of subsistence for birds and marine mammals.

A major nesting region and breeding ground, the Aleutian area is host for 183 species and subspecies of birds. Ducks and geese winter on many of the islands; eagles and falcons are permanent residents of most of the Chain; and many shorebirds, such as sandpipers, breed on the islands and the Peninsula.[4] It is mainly because of the wildfowl population that the Aleutians were established as a wildlife refuge in 1913.

Eighteen species of terrestrial mammals and twenty-one species of marine mammals have been reported in the Aleutians area. Of the terrestrial mammals, only the fox is thought to be native to the area, the others being introduced by man. Caribou were established on Adak Island in the 1950s, although they were known to have been on the eastern Aleutian Island of Unimak much earlier, and of course they are also present on the Alaska Peninsula. Reindeer were introduced to Atka Island in 1914, and even earlier on Unalaska. Most of the islands are inhabited by foxes (mainly red and blue), although trapping has proved economically

---

[3]
  Ibid., p. 158.
[4]
  Ibid., pp. 181-86; WSR, pp. 143-68.

unfeasible since the late 1940s. Wolverines, weasels, land otter, mice, ground squirrels, and rats are also found in the area.[5] Moose and bears are also found on the Alaska Peninsula.[6]

Of the marine mammal population, the sea otter has been the most significant historically. It once inhabited the entire region, until decimated by Russian fur hunters in the eighteenth and nineteenth centuries. Today, the sea otter population is over 100,000, located mainly in the central Aleutians and Sanak Islands group. Another important sea mammal is the northern fur seal, which breeds on the Pribilof Island rookeries and which has been significant economically since the discovery of the Pribilofs in the 1780s. Also found in the Aleutians are northern sea lions, harbor seals, walrus, and at least seven species of whales.[7]

Fish form another important aspect of the Aleutian environment. Freshwater streams throughout the Aleutians provide spawning areas for sockeye, chum, pink, and coho salmon, and the waters of the area are used by great numbers of migrating salmon.[8] The eastern Aleutians and Alaska Peninsula have been significant historically, and are still extremely important, as salmon fishing grounds. Much of the area's economic importance in the twentieth century lies in this aspect of the environment.

---

[5] WSR, pp. 169-71.

[6] SW Regional Profile, p. 189.

[7] WSR, pp. 171-95.

[8] Ibid., pp. 197-203; pp. 200-203 of this Report list seventy-five different inshore fishes collected at Amchitka Island as an indication of the diversity and production of the area.

Too often the Aleutian region has been the target of bad publicity due to its environment. Titles of the more popular books about the area--such as T.P. Bank's Birthplace of the Winds, Isobel Hutchinson's Stepping Stones from Alaska to Asia, Murray Morgan's Bridge to Russia: Those Amazing Aleutians, Simeon Oliver's Son of the Smoky Sea, and Harold McCracken's Hunters of the Stormy Sea--either stress the Aleutians' strategic location in terms of world politics and world war, or bring to mind images of an area inhospitable to human habitation.[9] These images were strengthened--if not produced--by the attitudes of American servicemen stationed in the Aleutians during World War II and their sarcastic remarks concerning Aleutian winds, Aleutian mosquitoes, and Aleutian sunshine (or, more specifically, the lack thereof).[10]

The image of the Aleutians as a harsh, forbidding, inhospitable, almost barren environment is a somewhat misleading one, however, for this region supported a considerable human population for generations before European discovery of the islands. Perhaps the pre-contact Aleut population was not so great as the 20,000 estimated by the priest Ivan Veniaminov and other Russian explorers in the 1820s, but certainly it may

---

[9]
Titles are somewhat misleading; all of these works are more realistic in their descriptions of the area than their titles suggest.

[10]
See, for example, "The Aleutians: They are Barren Links Between Two Worlds," Life, 16 (March 13, 1944); 70-86, which describes the Islands as "wild" and "inhospitable"; and also "Repulsive is a GI Word Meaning the Aleutians," Newsweek, 26 (November 26, 1945); 63-65, wherein is written the remark that the Aleutians are comprised of "terrain where nothing existed that was needed by human life except fresh water."

have been the 15,000 estimated by today's anthropologists. [11] One of

these anthropologists, T.P. Bank, has written that "every island, no

matter how small, has contained native villages. Each bay, inlet, cove

and bight which affords protection from the worst storms was probably

inhabited at one or more times during the period of Aleut occupation of

the Aleutian Arc." [12]

It is undeniably because of, rather than in spite of, the Aleutian

environment that this occupation was possible. The Aleuts were well

adapted materially and socially to their maritime way of life. Numerous

sites were available for the establishment of villages--both permanent

settlements and seasonal camps. Fresh water was readily available on

many islands of the Aleutian Chain in ponds, lakes and streams. The

waters of the Aleutians, supplemented by the availability of wildfowl and

plant life, provided the necessary subsistence resources; the strong cur-

rents of the Bering Sea and Pacific Ocean even supplied some--never

enough--driftwood for construction purposes. Indeed, the products of

the Aleutian environment were what drew Russian traders to the area,

which in turn caused the eventual decline of the Aleut population. The

whole history of human acitvity in the Aleutian region has been of a sim-

ilar nature: the environment and the people have always been intertwined,

---

[11]
Margaret Lantis, "The Aleut Social System, 1750 to 1810, From Early Historical Sources," in Ethnohistory in Southwestern Alaska and the Southern Yukon; Method and Content, ed. by Margaret Lantis (Lexington: University of Kentucky Press, 1970): 139-301, p. 172.

[12]
Theodore P. Bank, II, "Ecology of Prehistoric Aleutian Village Sites," Ecology, 34(April, 1953): 247.

sometimes leading to the destruction of one, sometimes to the destruction of the other, but neither has ever been indifferent to the other.

II. ALEUTIAN ARCHAEOLOGY

In 1953 Albert C. Spaulding of the University of Michigan wrote that despite over eighty years of archaeological investigation in the area "detailed scientific archaeology in the Aleutians is in its infancy."[1] Almost twenty years later Allen P. McCartney similarly noted that "prehistoric inquiry in the island has been spotty at best," and that "Spaulding's conclusions regarding the state of Aleutian archaeology . . . still apply very well today."[2] There is an even greater dearth of information regarding the prehistory of the lower Alaska Peninsula and the Shumagin Islands.[3]

However meager the results--and they are not all that bad--the Aleutian Islands have intrigued archaeologists and archaeology-minded naturalists for over 100 years, and the history of archaeological research in the region has included some highly significant scientists, as

---

[1]
Albert C. Spaulding, "The Current Status of Aleutian Archaeology," Society for American Archaeology, *Memoirs*, 9(1953): p. 31.
[2]
Allen P. McCartney, "An Archaeological Site Survey and Inventory for the Aleutian Islands National Wildlife Refuge, Alaska, 1972;" unpublished report submitted to the Wilderness Studies Branch, U.S. Fish and Wildlife Service, Anchorage, Alaska, November 1, 1972, pp. 40, 41; hereafter cited as McCartney, "Aleutian Islands Survey."
[3]
Allen P. McCartney, "An Archaeological Site Survey and Inventory for the Alaska Peninsula, Shumagin Islands and Other Islands of the Alaska Peninsula, 1973;" unpublished report submitted to the Refuges Branch, U.S. Fish and Wildlife Service, Anchorage, Alaska, July, 1973, p. 2; herafter cited as McCartney, "Alaska Peninsula Survey."

well as provided equally significant theorizing about the early inhabitants of the Chain.

The first such scientist to be considered was William Healy Dall, who had been, between 1865 and 1867, a member of the Western Union Telegraph Extension's scientific corps and succeeded Robert Kennicott as leader of the WUTE Russian-American division. Following the abandonment of the telegraph project, Dall remained in the North to carry out scientific investigations, among these archaeological investigations conducted from Attu to the Alaska Peninsula and beyond, to Kodiak Island, in the early 1870s.

McCartney has noted the implications of the conclusions drawn by Dall from his Aleutian studies. Some of these conclusions have been supported by more recent work in the area: the Aleutian Islands were populated from east to west, in more than one migration, and were occupied for a considerable time span; midden evidence also suggested to Dall a gradual progression from Eskimo to historic Aleut traits without significant interruption. Other of Dall's assumptions--for instance, his breakdown of midden evidence into three stages of food staples and food procurement methods (Littoral, Fishing, and Hunting Periods), which were supposedly to have corresponded with developmental stages of the Aleut population--have been found to be erroneous by more recent researchers.[4]

---

[4]
McCartney, "Aleutian Islands Survey," pp. 32-33; William Healy Dall, "On Succession in the Shell-Heaps of the Aleutian Islands," in "Tribes of the Extreme Northwest," Contributions to North American Ethnology, Vol. 1 (Washington, D.C.: Government Printing Office, 1877): 41-106.

Although largely theoretical, and based on relatively little empirical data, Dall's work in the Aleutians deserves more than the criticism leveled at it by Spaulding: "Certainly no subsequent investigation has produced the slightest evidence to support Dall's conclusions."[5] Dall's early investigations were indeed significant, if only for the fact of their extensiveness at the time when they were carried out in relation to the state of the science of archaeology in the same period. Moreover, McCartney notes that "though some of Dall's reasoning proved to be deductively fallacious, he was the first to utilize ethnographic materials and information to interpret artifacts."[6]

Aside from Alphonse Louis Pinart's less extensive collection gathered from Aleutian burial caves in the 1870s, no more major archaeological work was done in the Aleutian Islands until the twentieth century, when Waldemar Jochelson, who led the anthropology section of the Imperial Russian Geographical Society's Aleutian-Kamchatka Expedition, spent nineteen months in 1909-1910 investigating thirteen village sites on the islands of Attu, Atka, Umnak, and Unalaska. In coordination with the archaeological work, ethnographic and linguistic research was also conducted.

The major conclusions resulting from Jochelson's research denied much of Dall's earlier thoerizing. Rather than Dall's three-stage evolutionary process, Jochelson suggested that the earliest inhabitants of the centuries old Aleut sites were culturally not far removed from the

---

[5] Spaulding, "Current Status," p. 29.

[6] McCartney, "Aleutian Islands Survey," p. 33.

Aleuts living on the islands at the time of European contact. Cultural changes occurred, but were not as significant as the apparent cultural continuity. McCartney notes that "Jochelson's valuable monograph established Aleutian prehistory . . . and served as the major opus of Aleut prehistory until the post-war period. It still remains one of the most valuable sources for comparative midden material for the island chain."[7]

The next significant archaeological investigation in the Aleutians was conducted by Ales Hrdlicka for the Smithsonian Institution between 1936 and 1938. Hrdlicka's examinations "remain the most extensive of any in the Aleutians."[8] The results of this research were published in 1945, after Hrdlicka's death. While this publication is important in terms of ethnographic material, McCartney finds it disappointing archaeologically: "practically no information indicative of systematic excavations or analysis is given; no quantitative data on the numbers of artifacts for any particular site is offered nor are numbers of artifacts per excavation units or levels, profile maps, or treatment of stylistic changes through time or space."[9]

Based on skeletal differences, Hrdlicka constructed a dichotomy of Aleut cultural periods and physical types, pre-Aleut and Aleut. The latter were supposedly a later intrusion into the Aleutians, as the pre-Aleut material seemed to make up the majority of the midden strata. The pre-Aleut were dominant in the western Aleutians even after the Aleut

---

[7] Ibid., p. 34.

[8] Ibid., p. 35.

[9] Ibid.

population migration from the east only a few centuries prior to Russian discovery of the Islands. This is Hrdlicka's main contribution to Aleutian archaeology, although the artifacts he excavated have not been studied extensively to bear out all of his assertions.[10]

The World War II period is easy to characterize in terms of its effect on the development of Aleutian archaeology: it was extremely destructive. Military activities throughout much of the Chain disturbed many of the archaeological sites that were already known from previous investigations, as well as many more sites not previously discovered. Archaeological pot-hunting was also common among military personnel, and this sort of activity on Amchitka Island is described in graphic detail by Paul Guggenheim, who once worked under Hrdlicka and who was a first-hand observer of the destruction of the Amchitka sites.[11] Similar activities, as well as destruction caused by military construction, took place in other parts of the Aleutians, and led McCartney to comment that "archaeologists working for hundreds of years could not alter and damage the number of sites that World War II forces did in 5 years."[12]

After the war, two major archaeological research projects were carried out in the Aleutians. Theodore P. Bank II of the University of Michigan led expeditions between 1948 and the early 1950s, and these efforts were extended by Spaulding in 1962. The major excavations of

---

[10]
Ibid.
[11]
Paul Guggenheim, "An Anthropological Campaign on Amchitka," Scientific Monthly, 61(January, 1945): 21-32.
[12]
McCartney, "Aleutian Islands Survey," p. 36.

these researchers were at Unalaska and Amaknak (Bank), and on Agattu (Spaulding). Minor excavating was done on Attu, Tanaga, Adak, Atka, and Umnak. Bank's research contradicts Hrdlicka's two population theory, and suggests that "isolation along the linear archipelago might have allowed regional variations of a physical, linguistic and artifactual nature to develop from one ancestral stock, thus forming a kind of continuum from east to west."[13]

Also beginning in 1948, and continuing through a number of field seasons through the 1960s, William Laughlin and his associates concentrated their efforts on two sites--Chaluka midden, and Anangula Island core and blade site--in the Nikolski Bay region of Umnak Island. The Chaluka site has produced the greatest amount of artifactual evidence of any Aleutian site, and its great age makes Chaluka prehistory synonymous with eastern Aleutian prehistory. Laughlin agrees with Hrdlicka's population dichotomy, but calls these phases Paleo-Aleut and Neo-Aleut-- rather than Hrdlicka's pre-Aleut and Aleut--to stress the continuity of Aleut culture in the area.[14]

Continuing research has been conducted in many areas of the Aleutians, although it would be difficult to describe any of this research as "major" investigations such as those of Dall, Hrdlicka, and Laughlin. Some of the more recent work, however, has provided some significant additional information for the study of Aleut prehistory.

For instance, the 1969-1970 survey and excavations on Amchitka Island

_____

[13]
  Ibid., p. 39.
[14]
  Ibid., p. 38.

reported by R.J. Desautels, A.J. McCurdy, J.D. Flynn, and R.R. Ellis for the Atomic Energy Commission is perhaps the first complete survey of a fairly large island in the Aleutian Chain. It shows the extensive utilization of all areas suitable for living or for subsistence activities by the Native population.[15] A similar survey of Adak Island conducted in the summer of 1975 doubled the number of sites reported from a survey of the island made only two years before.[16]

The archaeological investigations on the lower Alaska Peninsula and the Shumagin Islands have been adequately characterized by McCartney:

> This region of southwestern Alaska . . . still remains a void on anthropological maps. Practically nothing about the early Peninsular Eskimo and Shumagin Aleut lifeways has been recorded since /Georg Wilhelm/ Steller's account /1741/. And information about the prehistoric period is still almost totally lacking. Systematic site surveys have been restricted to only the extreme ends of the Alaska Peninsula and essentially no literature is available for the larger central part of the Peninsula or the Pacific islands offshore.[17]

Archaeological investigations of the area in the nineteenth century are, as McCartney noted, almost entirely lacking, except for mummies and other artifacts gathered from a cave on Unga Island by Dall and Pinart.[18]

The Hot Springs site at Port Moller has perhaps provided the most significant archaeological data for the lower Alaska Peninsula in the

---

[15]
R.J. Desautels, et. al., Archaeological Report, Amchitka Island, Alaska, 1969-70 (U.S. Atomic Energy Commission, Division of Technical Information, 1971).

[16]
Bruno Frohlich found seventy-six sites on the island during the 1975 survey (Aleut Corporation Files); McCartney, "Aleutian Islands Survey," pp. 22-33 noted only thirty-eight sites on the island.

[17]
McCartney, "Alaska Peninsula Survey," p. 2.

[18]
Ibid., p. 5.

twentieth century. The site was first examined in 1928 by E.M. Weyer, again by William Workman in 1960, and by K. Kotani in 1972. Other archaeologists have utilized the Port Moller material in comparison with other work done on the Alaska Peninsula to develop theories for delineating the Aleut-Eskimo boundary on the Peninsula.[19]

In the late 1930s Hrdlicka compiled information concerning prehistoric and historic sites on the Peninsula and the offshore islands. McCartney has also done considerable survey work in this area, as well as archaeological excavations at Izembek Lagoon, on the northwestern coast of the Peninsula.

As can be seen, systematic excavation, survey, and analysis of findings in the Aleutians and on the Alaska Peninsula have largely taken place since the end of World War II. Yet despite McCartney's strictures that Spaulding's conclusions of 1953 concerning the voids in Aleutian archaeology can still apply today, great advances have been made. These advances are in regard both to regional sequences within the Aleutians, as well as in regard to the Aleutians' place in the prehistory of Alaska in general.

Most of the theorizing concerning the earliest prehistory of the Aleutians is based on archaeological evidence gathered from two eastern Aleutian sites, Chaluka and Anangula. The Chaluka site, on Nikolski Bay of Umnak Island, shows continual occupation of the area for 4,000 years. The bone and stone artifacts, as well as faunal material gathered at the

---

[19]
    Don E. Dumond, Leslie Conton, and Harvey M. Shields, "Eskimos and Aleuts on the Alaska Peninsula: A Reappraisal of Port Moller Affinities," Arctic Anthropology, 12(1975): 49-67.

site, indicate a population already adapted to a maritime environment.

Even older is the Anangula Island (off the coast of Umnak) site, a microblade manufacturing area and village site occupied approximately 8,000 years ago, when Anangula Island formed the southwestern end of the Alaska Peninsula. It is thought that at about this period "coastal people from Asia drifted along the southern perimeter of the Bering Land Bridge to its southwest corner, now known as Umnak, and over the next several thousand years, drifted further west to the end of the 1,100-mile chain of the Aleutians."[20]

From archaeological evidence gathered from various portions of the Aleutian Islands, cultural continuity over a great period of time seems the most striking feature, and few discontinuities have been found throughout the Chain. A distinctive "Near Island Phase" noted by McCartney may be due only to the isolation of this western group from the rest of the Aleutian Islands--almost 200 miles separates the Near Island group from the next eastern group--and even the differences here "are only stylistic and superficial when compared to the strong common cultural base in which they shared."[21]

Cultural continuity of the Aleut population over such a considerable period of time throughout the Aleutian Islands leads to some interesting problems in the relationship between archaeological theories of the last twenty years and the sporadic nature of Aleutian archaeology. For instance, most Aleutian archaeological investigations have focused on

---

[20]
   WSR, p. 47.
[21]
   Ibid., p. 49.

portions of the eastern Aleutians, and in areas adjacent to present-day Aleut villages. Only further, more intensive surveys and systematic excavations throughout the Chain can evaluate and elucidate the regional diversities that are known to exist in Aleut adaptations to the Aleutians environment in areas such as settlement and subsistence patterns, and other aspects of Native life.

In terms of settlements, for instance, it is known--particularly from research done in the eastern Aleutians--that Aleut settlement systems were characterized by base villages utilizing seasonal satellite camps. More intensive surveys of different Aleutian regions can greatly increase knowledge of the extent of this pattern within a given area, as well as between different island groups. As an example, the Aleutian survey conducted by McCartney in 1972 for the <u>Aleutian Islands Wilderness Study Report</u> noted a total of thirty-eight Native settlement sites on Adak Island; the survey of Adak conducted in 1975, however, located another thirty-eight sites on the island. Similarly, the 1969-1970 investigations on Amchitka Island found seventy-six village or camp sites on that island. The large number of sites found on these two islands in only the last few years form more of an indication of the nature of Aleutian archaeological surveys, rather than an indication of the extent of Native utilization of these areas for settlement or subsistence purposes. Future surveys of other islands and, more importantly, complete surveys of whole island groups, may indicate similar extensive utilization of all areas which provided access to subsistence resources. Also, such surveys can point out which areas were not so extensively utilized, and environmental and archaeological research combined could help determine the requirements necessary for Aleut utilization of an area over time.

A similar situation can be found in diversities in subsistence utilization. From early Russian sources it is known that Aleut settlements were generally located on the northern coasts of the islands, due to the greater abundance of resources found on the Bering Sea Coasts. On Amchitka, however, there are an equal number of sites on both the northern and southern coasts of the island. Further research can help determine what resources were actually utilized on the Pacific Ocean and Bering Sea coasts of the Aleutians. Investigation of regional (inter-island as well as intra-island) differences in the presence, absence, and abundance of subsistence resources can also help determine the changes in, or continuity of, Aleut cultural adaptations throughout the Chain.

Research conducted on the lower Alaska Peninsula has found a different sort of settlement and subsistence utilization pattern, due mainly to environmental factors. The terrain on the northern coast of the Peninsula limits the areas suitable for permanent settlements to about 10% of the region. However, abundant subsistence resources allow for the area's heavy exploitation by a maritime population using short-term camps. Also, most archaeological material on the Peninsula, as well as on the islands of the Peninsula's southern coast, does not appear to be very old. Perhaps the most significant aspect of research in this area is the finding of close cultural ties between material gathered from the Shumagin Islands and from the portions of the Peninsula that have been tested.[22] The significance of future research in this area lies in clarifying the implications of this material--determining and delineating the nature and

---

22

McCartney, "Alaska Peninsula Survey," pp. 10, 13.

extent of cross-cultural ties between the Aleuts, peninsular Eskimo, and Koniag Eskimo, all three of which interacted in this region.[23]

All this is to say that although great advances have been made since World War II in the understanding and explanation of Aleut prehistory through archaeological investigations, the work that has been done is only a beginning. More questions seem to have been raised than answered, and only further surveys and excavations--on a systematic basis--can better delineate the patterns of Aleut life as it existed in the Aleutians and on the Alaska Peninsula prior to European contact with these areas.[24]

[23]
    Dumond, et. al., "Eskimos and Aleuts," p. 58.
[24]
    I am grateful to Doug Veltre of the University of Alaska, Anchorage for his personal communication regarding the significance of Aleut Archaeological sites in delineating the broader picture of life in the Aleutians.

III. ETHNOLOGICAL CONSIDERATIONS

They were four dreary, backbreaking days into the month of September, 1741, more than a month since the explorers' first landfall off the southern coast of Alaska. The ever changing weather was clear again, after alternating between drizzles, heavy rain, fog, and terrible squalls for weeks. The two-masted ship, St. Peter, had been anchored off the two islands for seven days, the crew--both sick and well--filling its casks with vitally needed water. The Captain Commander of the Russian expedition, Vitus Bering, was already suffering from the scurvy which was to kill him three months later, while the first of the expedition's sailors to die, Nikita Shumagin, memorialized with his name the island group on which he was buried.

On the first night after their landfall in the Shumagins, the Russians had seen a fire on the shore of the larger of the islands, later to be named Nagai. For the next few days a party under Fleet Master Sophron Khitrov, carrying trinkets as gifts for the natives, went out in search of the "Americans." The German-born naturalist, Georg Wilhelm Steller, ashore with the water party, had to be content with observing the plant and animal life of Nagai Island, while he unsuccessfully attempted to convince his companions that the brackish water they were collecting would eventually prove hazardous to their health.

Then, for two days, the ship had been kept from the open sea by high, shifting winds, and late in the afternoon of September 4th the St. Peter approached the northern coast of Bird Island. The crew had barely dropped anchor when, according to Steller's journal,

> we heard a loud shout from the rocks to the south of us, which
> at first, not expecting any human beings on this miserable
> island . . . , we held to be the roar of a sea lion. A little
> later, however, we saw two small boats paddling toward our
> vessel from shore. We all waited for them with the greatest
> eagerness and full of wonder in order, on the arrival of these
> islanders, to pay special attention to their appearance and
> characteristics.[1]

Steller and his journal were not to reach Kamchatka, from whence
the expedition had sailed, for almost an entire year, yet as the first
trained naturalist in the Aleutian Islands his notations of the "appear-
ance and characteristics" of the first Aleuts encountered by the Russian
explorers comprise the earliest attempt at describing at least some aspects of Aleut culture to the European scientific community.

Despite the brief period of time Steller had to observe the Aleuts--
he saw them twice in two days--before the wind shifted and the St. Peter
was able to get to sea again, the naturalist was able to write much of
what he saw in his journals. He described the bidarkas of the Aleuts in
some detail, as well as Aleut clothing and items of personal decoration.
He made comparisons between Aleut dress and ornamentation with that of
the natives of eastern Siberia. He also decided, probably correctly,
that these natives did not inhabit the Shumagin islands, but only spent
their summers there to gather birds' eggs, large numbers of which he had

---

[1]
    Steller's journal is in Frank A. Golder, Bering's Voyages; an Account
of the Efforts of the Russians to Determine the Relation of Asia and
America, 2 vols. (reprint of 1825 edition; New York Octagon Books,
Inc., 1968), 2:90.

observed on the island.[2]

Following more extensive activities of Russian fur traders in the Aleutians in the later 1740s, and the resulting more intimate contact with the native inhabitants of the islands, further information regarding Aleut life and culture made its way into print. Most of this information did not come directly from the fur traders, although reports of relations between Aleuts and traders did filter back to St. Petersburg at a rate to allow some government interest in and inquiries into--if not direct regulation of--trading activities.

Instead, most data which might merit the name of ethnographic information came from the journals of the continuing voyages of discovery, and the more literate leaders of trading expeditions. This information was often published (somewhat after the fact; reports of early Russian exploratory efforts were not widely distributed until the 1770s), either as complete volumes of these voyages, or as articles in scientific publications, such as Peter Simon Pallas' articles in his seven volume work on the geography and natural history of various remote portions of the Russian Empire.[3] Very often these items were picked up by interested authors in other countries (such travel accounts and studies of natural history were

---

[2]
Ibid., pp. 90-105. Alexei Chirikov, who was Bering's second-in-command and commanded the St. Paul, also met Aleuts, off Adak Island, in September on his way back to Kamchatka; see Ibid., 1:303-5. The journals of the St. Paul's voyage do not give as complete a description of the Aleuts as does Steller's.

[3]
James R. Masterson and Helen Brower, Bering's Successors, 1745-1780; Contributions of Peter Simon Pallas to the History of Russian Exploration Toward Alaska (Seattle: University of Washington Press, 1948).

tremendously popular in the enlightened eighteenth and nineteenth centuries, not only among scholars, but among the lay readership as well), whose compilations were translated, published, and further plagiarized throughout Europe.

Most of the explorer's reports on Aleut culture suffer, however, because of the short time usually available to these travelers for observations of Native life. Generally, one finds in these accounts primarily descriptions of Aleut physical and material culture clothing, ornamentation, tools, housing, methods of hunting--or the more interesting, amusing, or outrageous customs which were observed. Aleut culture as such, or what Margaret Lantis calls "the system that held all the customs together,"[4] was either not observed, or, more likely, not understood. Still, the information these reports provide is invaluable, especially for the late eighteenth and early nineteenth centuries, before that culture was unalterably changed--particularly the changes due to relocation and population decline--through Russian contact.

Lantis divided the explorers' and scientists' reports on Aleut life into five periods. Although these reports do not always fall as "naturally" into these divisions as Lantis insists, the divisions are useful in delineating the major interests of the writers involved with disseminating information about the Aleuts after European discovery of the Aleutian Islands. The divisions are also useful in Lantis' development of a composite look at Aleut cultural life as it changed through time.

The initial period which Lantis discusses (1755-1785) is character-

---

[4] Lantis, "Aleut Social System," p. 144.

ized by the reports of explorations--such as those of Krenitsin and
Levashev in the 1760s, and that of Captain Cook in the next decade--and
the compilations edited by Gerhard Müller (1758), Pallas (1781-83), and
the unknown J.L.S., who wrote the standard work on Aleutian discoveries
in 1776, which was translated into English by William Coxe in 1780.
Most of these reports are short, and typify the authors' interest in the
unusual, rather than in cultural systems. These reports discuss, however,
Aleut relations with their early white visitors, "and provide a starting
point for the study of interethnic relations and culture change."[5]

The next period (1785-1810) Lantis characterizes as one of great
change in the "scientific value" of the reports produced. Certainly the
expeditions were more ambitious, such as the Geographical and Astronomi-
cal Expedition to the Northeast Parts of Russia (1785-1791) commanded by
Captain Joseph Billings. The reports of this expedition, particularly
those of Gavril Sarytchev, Martin Sauer, and Carl Merck "begin to sound
like modern scientific reports," and contain significant information on
Aleut settlement patterns in the Islands visited.[6] In this period also
is the Russian round-the-world expedition reported by its commanders
Ivan Krusenstern and Yuri Lisianski, as well as the expedition physician
Georg Heinrich von Langsdorff's report on Unalaska and the Pribilof
Islands.

Lantis' next period, 1815-1855, shows a continuation of explorers'
reports, such as von Kotzebue's 1815-1818 and 1823-1826 voyages,
Khromchenko's explorations of 1821-1833, and Litke's voyage of 1826-1829.

---

[5]
 Ibid., p. 150.
[6]
 Ibid., pp. 151, 152.

24

More significant, however, is the fact that this period produced the reports of those who came to the Aleutians not to explore and exploit in the shortest amount of time, but also those who remained in the Islands long enough to provide more meaningful descriptions of Aleut culture. Prominent among these was Ivan Veniaminov, the Russian Orthodox priest who was later to become Bishop of Alaska. He arrived on Unalaska Island in 1825 and remained there for ten years, a stay which resulted in his three-part Notes on the Unalaska Islands District, published in St. Petersburg in 1840, the first true ethnographic study of the Aleuts. Descriptions of Aleut life and culture can also be found in the reports of other Russian Orthodox priests in this period and later, some of which have at least been partially translated.

The next period Lantis discusses is that between 1870 and 1915, after the American purchase of Alaska. Late nineteenth-century naturalists who concerned themselves with the Aleuts include Alphonse Pinart, whose field notes (in German, French, Russian, and English) of work in the Aleutian Islands in 1871-1872 contain information on Aleut religion, mythology, and linguistics. At about the same period, Dall was conducting his archaeological investigations of the Aleutians. In the later 1870s, Ivan Petroff was in the Aleutians gathering material for H.H. Bancroft's History of Alaska. One of Petroff's major contributions is his journal of this trip (which he also utilized in writing his description of Alaska and its resources for the 1880 census), which discusses some of the changes the Aleuts had undergone after almost 150 years of contact with Europeans and Americans. In the first decade of the twentieth century Frank Golder published a number of articles containing Aleut songs and stories, while a few years later Jochelson's anthropological work in the

25

Aleutians resulted in his History, Ethnology, and Anthropology of the Aleut, although in terms of ethnology "the principal value of the work is the kinship terminology."[7]

Lantis lastly analyzes the period 1930- Present (1970). The first major work of this period was Hrdlicka's investigation in the Aleutians in the late 1930s. Although primarily archaeological in orientation, Hrdlicka's publication, The Aleutian and Commander Islands and Their Inhabitants, is also a compilation of excerpts of the major ethnographic notes from the literature on the Aleuts. Particularly important are the notes, from Veniaminov and others, on population statistics and the location of early villages, as well as information on Aleut society and culture. These notes are usefully divided into Hrdlicka's discussions of specific islands and island groups he visited. Lantis herself was also active in this period, collecting information concerning Aleut ethnology in 1933 and 1934 on Atka Island.

During World War II little ethnographic information was gathered, as the Aleuts of the greater part of the Chain were relocated in southeast Alaska (it is unfortunate that this opportunity for significant studies of Aleut culture change was seemingly ignored). However, the records comprising the "Pribilof Islands Logbooks," copies of which are in the University of Alaska archives, are excellent (although not the only) sources of information on how a portion of the Aleut population was affected by this relocation.

Following the war, Gerald Berreman's research on Umnak goes into

---

[7] Ibid., p. 167.

some detail on the present Aleut social system, and the significance of culture change in Aleut life. At the same time Bank's archaeological and ecological studies resulted in a more popular account of Aleut society as it existed after the Aleuts returned to their islands (particularly Unalaska) after the war. Although Lantis does not go into detail, the work of Knut Bergsland in the field of Aleut linguistics in the early 1950s has significance far beyond the analysis of Aleut dialects. As part of that analysis Bergsland used data provided by Aleut informants who were knowledgeable about place names throughout the western Islands. This sort of information has not been used as much as it could (or should) be to help delineate Aleut settlement patterns, subsistence resource utilization, and even Aleut mythology. The potential for further work along these lines exists, and Aleut hunters are still utilizing many portions of the Aleutian chain which have long been uninhabited.

Lantis' discussion of sources for composing an ethnology of the Aleutians ends here, in the late 1940s-early 1950s. Little original research in this field seems to have been done since that time, as the major concentration of anthropologists in the Aleutians seems to be archaeological in orientation, due primarily to the interesting research done by Laughlin and the resulting desire to fill out the outlines of Aleut prehistory. There have been, however, continued reprintings of the more important journals of Russian and other European exploratory voyages, and some articles on present-day medical and social problems in the Aleutians contain information on early Aleut society gleaned from the older sources. And, of course, in 1970 Lantis compiled the ethnohistorical material she discussed into a study of Aleut society as it probably existed just prior to and through the major period of Russian contact.

Lantis concentrates on the nonmaterial aspects of Aleut culture. In general categories she discusses changes in Aleut population size, the physical make-up of the Aleut village, Aleut housing, something of the daily activities within the family and the wider relationships within the village. On a more individual level, she discusses the "crises of life"--Aleut customs relating to birth, puberty, marriage, and death. She then goes into a detailed account of the Aleut social system, particularly kinship and social and personal relationships within the family. Lantis concludes with a study of political authority, systems of justice, warfare, trade, and, finally, the breakdown of Aleut culture under Russian domination.

Population statistics for the Aleuts at the time of Russian contact are of course unavailable. Such statistics were not reported by Russian explorers until nearly thirty years after initial contact, after the drastic decline in Aleut population had already begun. Also, some explorers counted both men and women, while some counted only the adult men in the villages they visited, or sometimes only families they found in these villages. Moreover, the nature of Aleut subsistence utilization, with the shifting of populations from base villages to seasonal camps, precluded exact examination, and by the time Russian traders had relocated Aleut village populations into larger villages so as to better control Aleut hunters, and others were taken to the farthest extremes of the area of the Russian fur trade, the population was already decimated.

According to Lantis' reading of the sources, a late eighteenth-century Aleut village was usually comprised of two or three large houses with three to ten nuclear families (20-30 people) per house. Lantis figures that a "reasonable" population estimate would be 12,000, with a maximum of 15,000 at the time of Russian contact. By the mid-1820s, when Veniaminov was

collecting his information on Unalaska, the situation had changed dra-

matically. Lantis estimates that "at least 80 percent of the Aleut pop-

ulation was lost in the first two generations of Russian contact." This

loss was due to the relocation of Aleuts to areas outside the Aleutian

Islands, as well as to death. It is mainly because of this population

decline that the early explorers' reports on the Aleutian Islands are so

important for delineating Aleut culture, for "by 1825 Aleuts were describ-

ing to their ethnographer, Veniaminov, a culture that was largely of the

past, a memory culture."[9]

According to Veniaminov, most Aleut villages were located on the

northern coasts of the islands, because of the greater abundance of sub-

sistence resources available along the edge of the Bering Sea. It is dif-

ficult to ascertain the accuracy of this observation. By the time

Veniaminov was writing his description of Aleut life, most of the Islands'

Natives had been relocated by the Russian-American Company into relative-

ly large villages which generally were on the northern coasts of the

islands. This may not be a good indication of aboriginal settlement pat-

perns. Moreover, recent surveys have found numerous settlement sites on

the southern coasts--indeed, on all coasts--of the Aleutian Islands, al-

though further research must be done to determine which were permanent

---

8
    Ibid., p. 174; it is difficult to determine population size by
remains of housepits located on Aleut archaeological sites, as not all
villages, nor even all housepits within a village, were inhabited at
the same time.
    9
    Ibid., p. 179.

village sites and which were used as seasonal camps. In any case, Jochelson has given a good description of the location of Aleut villages:

> All the ancient Aleut villages were situated on the seashore, . . . and usually on land between two bays, so that their skin boats could easily be carried from one body of water to another at the approach of foes. Thus the usual location of villages was on narrow isthmuses, on necks of land between two ridges, on promontories, or narrow sandbanks /all these are fairly common attributes of the coastlines of many of the Aleutian Islands/. An indispensable adjunct to a village was a supply of easily accessible fresh water--a brook, fall, or lake. . . . Near every village was an observatory . . . on a hill where constant watch was kept. . . . Here, too, hunters watched for the appearance of sea mammals, and in turn the people of the village watched for the return of the hunters.[10]

Almost all the early visitors to the Aleutians mentioned the Aleuts' housing, semi-subterranean barabaras, varying in size according to the number of families inhabiting each unit. Veniaminov noted that on Unalaska between ten and forty families would occupy houses which were between 60 and 180 feet long, and 24 to 54 feet wide.[11] These houses were sunk partially underground, and constructed of driftwood and whalebone covered with grass and moss, while a hole in the roof provided entry. They were heated by the use of stone lamps. Sometimes the houses would have small side rooms. No mention was made of Aleut sweathbaths, or of the larger ceremonial houses noted later among Eskimo villages on the Alaskan mainland.

Although admitting that the early information which is available

---

[10]
Waldemar Jochelson, Archaeological Investigations in the Aleutian Islands, Carnegie Institute of Washington Publication No. 367 (Washington, D.C.: Government Printing office, 1925), p. 23.
[11]
Lantis, "Aleut Social System," p. 187.

lacks explicit detail, Lantis interprets these reports as indicating ma-
trilineal descent among the Aleuts, with either matrilocal or matripatri-
local residence: "The household comprised a man and his wife or wives,
his older married sons and their families, and perhaps a younger brother
and family."[12] A boy's training was carried out by his mother's brother.
Marriages were generally arranged by parents, and cross-cousin marriages
were preferred. A man could have as many wives as he could support, although one or two seems to have been the most common number by the mid-
nineteenth century. Men married at thirteen or fourteen, and the family
would generally move to the home of the husband's family after the birth
of their first child.

Men hunted, fished, built the wooden frames for the bidarkas, com-
posed and sang the songs used in ceremonies, and did some carving--ivory
figures and decorations, as well as the stone sealoil lamps. Women
cleaned fish in summer, collected berries and roots, sewed clothing and
the skin covering of the bidarkas. At times, women also danced in the
ceremonies.[13]

The aspect of Aleut culture which seems to have been most interesting to early visitors to the Aleutians, and one which they invariably
discussed at length, was the Aleuts' method of disposing of their dead.
Particularly interesting was the way in which Aleuts mummified some of
the bodies. The degree of care taken over the remains of the dead generally depended on a number of factors: "The rank of the individual,

---

[12]
  Ibid., pp. 227, 292-93.
[13]
  Ibid., pp. 194-95.

circumstances of his death, season in which the death occurred, and local preferences probably all contributed to determining when a person should be buried in a house compartment, in a cave, or in a coffin". For example, "in the eastern and middle Aleutians, merely placing the body in a cave was the least respectful way of disposing of it, but placing a carefully mummified and wrapped body in a frame and then secreting it in a cave with an accompanying deposit of goods (and sometimes also the body of a slave) was the most honorable."[14] Mourning practices were also often commented upon, especially the mourning period for a child, which could last for over a year, during which time the body would be kept in the barabara, perhaps in one of the side rooms.

Compared to observations on death practices, the information regarding the Aleuts' customs surrounding birth and marriage is meager, although Lantis discusses the major ceremonies connected with these times of life.[15]

Less attention has been paid in most studies of the Aleuts to the structure of their society. According to Veniaminov and other observers, Aleut society was divided into three classes. On top was what might be termed a nobility, a fairly large group, although true "chieftainship" was available to only a small percentage. The second group was comprised of the common people, a middle class, which seems not to have been a very large group at all, but from which people could only rarely rise into the upper class. On the bottom of the social ladder were the slaves,

---

[14]
   Ibid., pp. 215, 217.
[15]
    Ibid., pp. 197-204.

generally prisoners of war, who could be freed or ransomed.

Wealth was generally tied to class. An island chief was entitled to a share of each village's hunt, and the members of the upper class could obtain more wealth through the sale of slaves, or through trade. The upper class could also generally afford to support more wives, which also raised their status, and a wealthy man could also afford--or would be given--burial and memorial feasts of great distinction. Generosity, such as giving away slaves, was also a sign of social status.

In terms of political authority and the administration of justice, Lantis writes:

> There was a tendency to inheritance of chieftainship although the higher chief for a group of villages or a whole island was chosen from among the lesser chiefs. /Consideration was generally given to successful--and thereby generous--hunters, and to those adept and brave in warfare./ Beyond one island there was no authority--only the duties of a kindred, and these might be divisive. Before the Discovery, there were feuds between kindreds: insults, raids, and murders being avenged. The formal accusations, hearings, and pronouncements of sentences that Aleuts were later reported to have had probably came after the Russian invasion.[16]

Shamanism was practiced among the Aleuts, particularly in regard to aiding hunting parties, and secret men's societies are also evident in many of the early observations of the Aleuts. Curing was another important aspect of Aleut shamanism, and Aleuts were well known for their curing skills and knowledge of anatomy, even practicing acupuncture. They also used numerous roots and herbs for healing.[17]

---

[16] Ibid., p. 295.

[17] Ibid., pp. 242, 244; Leda Chase Milan, "Ethnohistory of Disease and Medical Care Among the Aleut," _Anthropological Papers of the University of Alaska_, 16 (August, 1974):17-18.

Warfare and trade seem to have been important aspects of Aleut culture before contact with Europeans. Kin responsibilities and protection of honor resulted in feuds, generally between families. Also, Aleut folklore contains many examples of raids between the various island groups.[18] Such warfare resulted in the taking of booty, incuding prisoners for slaves, and would lead to retaliatory raids. European observers of Aleut warfare concluded that success in these operations was usually the result of "stratagems and deceits," each side taking advantage of opportunities of surprise and ambush; this often seemed unmanly to Europeans.[19] Warfare was also carried on between the Aleuts of the eastern Aleutians and the Kodiak Eskimo and Eskimo of the Alaska Peninsula.

Trade seems to have been highly developed among the Aleuts. This trade was mainly between contiguous villages, inter-island trade being relatively uncommon. The Aleuts dealt mainly in items such as masks, bracelets, parkas and other items of clothing, dentalium, amber, sea otter skins, and sometimes slaves and hunting equipment. Such trade was usually carried out by a middleman who bartered between the owner of an item and a prospective buyer until agreement was reached on a price.[20]

What heightens the significance of a discussion of Aleut life and culture as it existed in the late eighteenth and early nineteenth centuries--as well as explaining the considerable difficulty in arriving at

---

[18]
Knut Bergsland, "Aleut Dialects of Atka and Attu," American Philosophical Society, Transactions, 49(No. 3, 1959):62-64.
[19]
Lantis, "Aleut Social System," pp. 268-69.
[20]
Ibid., pp. 272-76.

an accurate picture of that culture from the observations of people not trained in the nuances of ethnographic description--are the changes undergone by the Aleuts due to intensive, and sometimes violent, contact with another culture (European) at the very time these observations were made. As noted earlier, Aleut population size and settlement patterns were particularly hard-hit because of the requirements and results of the sea otter trade. But these are only the more obvious manifestations of what Lantis calls the "extreme stress" that caused the breakup of Aleut culture at this time.[21]

Lantis discusses four major manifestations of this stress. The major stress was the loss of population, which Lantis estimates as probably four-fifths between 1741 and 1820. This depopulation was due in part to disease, and to a greater extent--how much will never be known--due to the activities, and sometimes atrocities, of the Russian fur traders. These atrocities lead to Lantis' second type of stress: "The Aleuts learned that they could not by themselves oppose the rapacious fur hunters and traders. It was only after the Russians had brought some order among themselves that the Aleuts were saved from the worst tyrannies. . . . There was no satisfaction of triumph or maintenance of independence to offset the loss of population, the breakup of communities."[22]

Third, according to Lantis, was the stress caused by the transportation and relocation of Aleut hunters to the east as Russian trading activities very quickly depleted the sea otter population. This quickened

---

21
   Ibid., p. 277.
22
   Ibid.

the breakup of communities and families, and resulted in the next area of
stress: Aleut men "lost self-confidence and lost control of their homes
while the women lived with 'Russians.' . . . The loss of morale . . .
must have been not only personally but socially demoralizing."[23] Finally,
with the coming of Russian priests by the early nineteenth century, the
Aleuts' own religion could not be maintained to unify Aleut society.

Some aspects of Aleut culture survived the disastrous effects of the
early Russian fur trade period, particularly in technology, art, and
ritual. Mostly, however, the rule from the beginning of Russian contact
was change, especially in the structures of family and society, and also
in religion. Also, the development of a new "class" in Aleut society--
the half-breed creoles who "served as communicators, translators of each
culture to the bearers of the other culture "[24] --was a tremendously power-
ful force for the undermining of the old Aleut way of life, and its re-
placement with something new.

Unfortunately, Lantis' study concludes with the end of the early
Russian fur trading period, and no ethnologists have provided as complete
a study of changing Aleut culture in later periods. Perhaps the closest
thing to this type of study is Bank's popular account of Aleut life on
Unalaska after World War II, and the more recent work of Dorothy M. Jones
in the eastern Aleutians and Alaska Peninsula. Also interesting is
Gerald Berreman's article on Aleut assimilation, which serves as a con-
cluding statement regarding Aleut reaction to 200 years of contact with
other cultures, rather than an effort at constructing an Aleut

---

[24]
Ibid., p. 291.

ethnology.[25] These studies, however, only briefly discuss the changing culture of the Aleuts from the mid-nineteenth to the mid-twentieth centuries.

Information for a complete ethnology of this later period is available, however. Visitors still made occasional stops in the Aleutians throughout the nineteenth and early twentieth centuries, and their written observations could add to information gained from more traditional ethnographic research. Priests, government officials, teachers, Coast Guard personnel--all made observations of Aleut culture which can be utilized to develop a complete picture of the complexities of a changing culture in the Aleutian Islands, and, more importantly, help provide an interpretation as to how and why that culture changed over time.

---

[25]
Gerald D. Berreman, "Aleut Reference Group Alienation, Mobility, and Acculturation," in Deward E. Walker, ed., The Emergent Native Americans; a Reader in Culture Contact (Boston: Little, Brown and Company, 1972), pp. 532-49.

IV. CONSIDERATIONS ON ALEUT HISTORY

On the 27th of August, 1742 the hooker <u>St. Peter</u>, built from the remains of the ship of the same name, sailed into the port of Petropavlovsk on the southeastern coast of the Kamchatka Peninsula. Led by Lieutenant Sven Waxel, only forty-five of the original crew of seventy-seven were returning after almost six months at sea off the southern coast of Alaska, and another eight months shipwrecked on Bering Island, where at least nineteen of the dead, including Captain Commander Vitus Bering, lay buried.

Bering's entire crew had been thought dead. Alexai Chirikov, second-in-command of Bering's exploratory expedition, had arrived in Petropavlovsk nearly ten months earlier, and, as officials had despaired of hearing further of Bering's portion of the expedition, "great . . . was the joy of everybody over our delivereance and safe arrival."[1] Perhaps greater excitement was reserved for something that Bering's men brought with them from the Alaska coast and Commander Islands--furs, among them over 900 sea otter skins. As one early Russian source for the development of the fur trade noted, "the tales of Bering's companions excited even more their desire to enrich themselves through sea-otter skins," which were valuable items of trade between the Russians and Chinese.[2] And a nineteenth-

---

[1] Golder, <u>Bering's Voyages</u>, 2:186.

[2] Vasilii N. Berkh, <u>A Chronological History of the Discovery of the Aleutian Islands or the Exploits of Russian Merchants, With a Supplement of Historical Data on the Fur Trade</u>, trans. by Dmitri Krenov, ed. by Richard A. Pierce (Kingston, Ontario: Limestone Press, 1974), p. 1.

century historian has more vividly depicted the importance of the skins brought back from Bering's expedition:

> Call it science, or patriotism, or progress, there is this to be said about the first Russian discoveries in America--little would have been heard of them for some time to come if ever, had it not been for the beautiful furs brought back from Bering Island. . . . Siberia was still sufficient to satisfy the tsar for purposes of expatriation, and the Russians were not such zealots as to undertake conquest for the sake of conversion, and to make religion a cloak for their atrocities; hence, but for these costly skins, each of which proclaimed in loudest strains the glories of Alaska, the Great Land might long have rested undisturbed.[3]

Such a bountiful area could not be left undisturbed for long. In the summer of 1743, barely a year after the safe return of the remnants of Bering's crew, Emilion Bassof led a fur hunting expedition to Bering Island.[4] Two years later, these enterprizing hunters and traders reached the Near Islands of the western Aleutians. Thus began the last major imperial conquest of a previously unknown (to Europeans) region of North America.

The period of the Russian fur trade in Alaska is the first major theme that must be considered in a discussion of the history of the Aleutian Islands. Certainly it was the fur trade which was the first cause, and had the greatest effect, on the Aleut culture changes which began in the late eighteenth century and lasted beyond the end of the Russian period in 1867. And the major changes took place relatively quickly, due to the intensive nature of Russian exploitation of the is-

---

[3]
Hubert Howe Bancroft, History of Alaska, 1730-1885 (reprint of 1886 edition; Darien Conn.: Hafner Publishing Co., 1970), pp. 95-98.
[4]
Berkh, Chronological History, pp. 2-4; Bassof returned to Bering Island again in 1745, 1747, and 1749.

lands' fur resources.

According to Vasilii Berkh's chronology, written in the 1820s,
Russian fur hunters concentrated their efforts in the Commander and Near
Islands until 1749, when an expedition, which remained in the Aleutians
for four years, reached Atka Island, midway along the Aleutian Arc. By
1751 Russian traders seem to have reached the Fox Islands of the eastern
Aleutians, one group of traders having seemingly been shipwrecked on
Umnak; this portion of the Aleutians was not significantly exploited for
furs, however, until 1759 when Stepan Glotov commanded a group of traders
which wintered on Umnak and hunted sea otters there and on Unalaska. In
1761, says Berkh, the enterprizing Russians had reached the Alaska Peninsula and the islands off its southern coast, and by 1763 the search for
sea otters led them beyond the Aleutian area to Kodiak Island.[5]

The reason for the extensive spread of Russian activity into the
Aleutians in the first twenty years after Bering's voyage is certainly
not to be found in the curiosity of either the Russian traders or the
Russian imperial government; indeed, there were no more official government sponsored explorations to reach the area until 1767. Rather, the
Russians' hasty extension was due to the rapid exploitation of fur-bearing
animals. Berkh notes more than thirty major fur trading expeditions between 1745 and 1763, expeditions which brought back furs (mostly sea
otters, sea otter tails, blue fox, and fur seals) valued at over 2,500,000
rubles.[6] And it must be remembered that these private expeditions con-

---

[5]
  Ibid., pp. 4-36.
[6]
  Ibid., pp. 98-101.

tinued until the 1790s, that the fur seal rookeries of the Pribilof
Islands were not discovered until 1786, and that the highly lucrative
trade was carried on to an even greater extent and to greater profits by
the Russian-American Company, which began its monopoly in 1798.

The eastward thrust of the Russian fur trade and the concomitant
progressive discovery of the Aleutians took place particularly because of
the speed with which the fur resources of the area were exploited. Berkh
noted the significant factor which drew the traders from the Kuriles on
to the Commander Islands and eventually the Aleutians, the coast of the
Alaskan mainland, and even to California: "The . . . seafarers went so
far East, because the sea otters, sea lions and fur seals were moving
east. These animals, seeing that the newcomers were attacking them with
an incredible cruelty, left their native shores and moved to safer places."[7]
By the 1780s, even the fur resources of Cook Inlet had become too depleted
for the private merchants, and trade seemed to decline for a time before
the Russian-American Company took over.[8]

The extension of Russian discoveries into the Aleutians area, the
activities of fur traders and explorers, and the changes in Russian trading practices due to the nature of the environmental conditions in the
Aleutians would all be fascinating subjects for historical treatment in
themselves. Russian trading activities in the area, however, cannot long
be discussed without also discussing the original inhabitants of the islands, and how the fur trade affected their lives. Unfortunately, although
general histories of Alaska always discuss the basic outline of intercul-

_____

[7]Ibid., p. 76.

[8]Bancroft, History of Alaska, p. 251.

tural contact and its effects on both Aleuts and Russians, the nuances of such interaction have been studied relatively lightly.

As an example of the changing nature of the fur trade itself, and the relation of the changes within the trade to the Aleut population, Bancroft notes that at first the Russians either hunted for the furs themselves, or, more generally, traded beads, tobacco, and knives to the Aleuts who hunted the sea otters. Soon after the beginning of intensive Russian activities in the islands, however, the Russians found a more effective method of operation, especially after their treatment of the Aleuts made going out in small hunting parties dangerous:

> Either by force or by agreement with chiefs the Aleuts . . .
> were obliged to give hostages, generally women and children, to
> ensure the safety of their visitors, or performance of contract.
> They /Aleut hunters/ were thereupon given traps and sent forth
> to hunt for the season, while the Russians lived in indolent re-
> pose at the village, basking in the smiles of the wives and
> daughters, and using them also as purveyors and servants. When
> the hunters returned they surrendered traps and furs in exchange
> for goods, and the task-masters departed for another island to
> repeat their operation.[9]

This type of operation continued under the Russian-American Company up to the time of the American purchase of Alaska, although relations seem to have been more formalized in the later period, the Aleuts being employed by the various stations which the Company established on several of the islands.

The use of Aleut hunters in this manner led to what Bancroft called "something akin to slavery" for the Aleuts, as well as further decimation of the sea otter population. Furthermore, after a time the half-breed

---

[9]
Ibid., pp. 235-36.

creoles were also utilized as hunters, explorers, and station managers who opened up new territories for trade. This, in time, led to violence between Aleuts and other groups of Alaskan Natives with whom they came in contact. These other Native groups "allowed no opportunity to escape them for revenge upon the despised race, not thinking that the poor fellows were but helpless tools of the Russians."[10]

Another aspect of the developing Russian fur trade, at least in relation to changes in the Aleuts' way of life, is the major relocation of the Aleut population, especially after the Russian-American Company began its monopoly of the trade in the 1790s. The inhabitants of numerous small villages scattered throughout the Aleutian Islands were resettled into larger villages (which became the stations of the Russian-American Company) on several of the larger islands in order to control the activities of Native hunters and the women who provided these hunters and the Russian traders, as well as to provide better harbors for use by Russian vessels. This reduction in the number of smaller Aleut villages and the development of larger, permanent settlements seem to have been accomplished rather quickly, as Veniaminov, in the 1820s, made many notations regarding the dwindling number of villages all along the Aleutian Chain. Of course, the great decline in the Aleut population in the early years of the Russian fur trade facilitated this relocation program.

And, of course, there were Russian acts of violence against the Aleuts, and the resulting hostility of the Natives toward the fur traders. On that September day in 1741, after Bering's crew first observed the Aleuts

---

[10]
    Ibid., p. 238.

off the coast of Bird Island, a party consisting of the naturalist
Steller, a native interpreter from Siberia, and ten sailors tried to
follow the Aleuts ashore. The ship's boat could not land on the rocky
beach, but the interpreter and two others swam ashore, where the Aleuts
evinced so much curiosity toward the strangers that they would not allow
the Russians to return to the boat. The Aleuts then tried to drag the
boat ashore, and the outcome was described by Steller:

> as the islanders could not be dissuaded from their purpose by
> sign language, shots were fired simultaneously over their heads
> at the rocks from three muskets . . . , by which unheard-of
> occurrance they became so freightened that they all fell down
> on the ground as if hit by thunder. Our men ran at once through
> the water and got safely into the boat. . . . /The Aleuts7 at
> once rose up again, scolded us because we had rewarded their
> good intentions so badly, and waved their hands to us to be
> off quickly as they did not want us any longer. Some of them
> in getting up picked up stones and held them in their hands.[11]

This was only a premonition of worse events to follow; and they fol-
lowed quickly enough. The first trading expedition to reach the western
Aleutians was led by Nikolai Chuprof. Bypassing Attu Island, his ship
anchored off Agattu, a few miles to the southeast, on September 24, 1745.
Two days later, in almost a reenactment of Steller's experience four years
earlier, a party of traders under Chuprof landed on the island to search
for water. A group of Aleuts met the Russians, who gave the Natives some
gifts. The Aleuts then attempted to take one of the traders' muskets.
When the Russians refused, the Aleuts became angry, and tried to seize
the ship's boat, whereupon muskets were fired at the Natives, wounding
one in the hand.

---

[11]
    Golder, _Bering's Voyages_, 2:94-95.

The Russians returned to their ship, which made its way back to Attu, where even more ominous events were to occur. First, a few Aleuts on Attu were wounded in a scuffle with the traders. Then, in October, Chuprof sent Alexei Beliaief to explore the island. Beliaief "discovered several habitations with whose inhabitants he managed to pick a quarrel, in the course of which fifteen of the islanders were killed. Even the Cossak Shekhurdin, who had accompanied Beliaief, was shocked at such proceedings and went and told Chuprof, who said nothing, but merely sent the butchering party more powder and lead."[12]

This is a familiar story to anyone with even a slight reading knowledge of Russian-American history. Even more familiar are the stories of Feodor Soloviev's cruel retaliation in 1764 against Unalaska Aleuts who had killed a group of Russian traders two years earlier. Bancroft noted that "the bloodshed perpetrated by this band of avengers was appalling. A majority of all the natives connected with the previous attacks on the Russians paid with their lives for presuming to defend their homes against invaders." Estimates of the number of Aleuts killed by Soloviev run as high as 3,000.[13] In the same period, as retaliation for the same Aleut "offenses," Lieutenant Davydov apparently killed another 3,000 Aleuts, and Ivan Glotov "destroyed all the villages on the southern side of Umnak and the inhabitants of the islands of Samalga and the Four Mountains."[14]

---

[12]
  Bancroft, History of Alaska, p. 105.
[13]
  Ibid., p. 151.
[14]
  Milan, "Disease and Medical Care Among the Aleut," p. 19.

One of the major causes of Aleut-Russian hostility during the first twenty years of Russian activity in the Aleutians was the lack of effective Russian imperial control over the traders. One of the reasons for the Imperial edict extending Russian sovereignty over the Aleutian Islands and Alaska Peninsula in 1766 were the reports which filtered into St. Petersburg concerning the atrocities committed by traders against the Aleuts. Despite the good intentions of the Russian government, however, complete control over the private traders was never effective, and even the creation of the Russian-American Company monopoly--the establishment of which was urged partly on the basis of fairer treatment of the Natives involved in the fur trade--could not stop the abuses of power which resulted from the isolation of the far-flung Russian possessions. Certainly by the 1790s, what the Russians might have originally conceived of as the necessity of making examples out of certain portions of the Aleut population was becoming less necessary, for the Aleuts had by then been completely subjugated, and tied inexorably to the fur trade.

Although acts of violence accounted for a considerable reduction in the Aleut population in the early years after Russian contact, there were other factors also at work, and they became increasingly important in later years, especially after the Russian-American Company took over the trade. Large groups of Aleut hunters were lost through accident, or died of starvation. One ethnologist has noted that during Baranof's establishment of the Russian trading center at Sitka in 1798 and 1799 over 200 Aleut men died of starvation or by drowning; the Russian traders' insatiable desire for more and more furs and fur trading area led them to send their hired Aleut hunters on riskier expeditions through treacherous coastal waters.[15]

Disease caused a more significant decline in the Aleut population. Venereal disease was noted in the Aleutians at the time of Billings' expedition in the 1790s, and was a major cause of Aleut infertility and death by Veniaminov's time, only thirty years later; tuberculosis was widespread, and uncontrollable, by 1824; and a major smallpox epidemic broke out in 1837-38, killing almost 3,000 Aleuts.[16] These diseases not only affected Aleut social structure, settlement patterns, and population size, but also aided in the decline of shamanism among the Aleuts, and in the loss of faith in their religion, as the shamans were generally unable to cure the new diseases.

To return again to Russian violence: it is easy to exaggerate what have come to be commonly known as Russian "atrocities" against the Aleuts in the fur trade period, as historians have too often done. The exact number of deaths which can be blamed on Russian traders will never be known; traders were certainly not eager for acts of cruelty to be reported to superiors either in Russian America itself, or back home in St. Petersburg. Yet however unpardonable the actual facts are, it is hardly accurate to say that the "Russians systematically slaughtered the hardy Aleuts,"[17] thereby implying that the killing of Aleuts was as planned a part of trading activities as was the killing of sea otters. Certainly

---

[15] Ibid.

[16] Ibid., pp. 20-21; Winston L. Sarafian, "Smallpox Strikes the Aleuts," Alaska Journal, 7 (Winter, 1977):49.

[17] Mary Clay Berry, The Alaska Pipeline: The Politics of Oil and Native Land Claims (Bloomington: Indiana University Press, 1975), p. 12.

not all Russian traders killed all the Aleuts they came across, and
Russian actions should not be (although they have been) labelled
"genocide."[18]   Bancroft hedged the issue; he wrote that the Aleuts were
"held in subjugation," and, more emotionally, that the shots fired at the
Aleuts on Agattu in 1745 inaugurated the Russians' "reign of violence
and bloodshed" in the Aleutians. Yet Bancroft later tempered these crit-
icisms of the Russians:

> The Russians were not in reality as cruel as the others
> /Europeans with whom the Aleuts later had dealings/, and above
> all, . . . they assimilated more closely with the aborigines
> than did other traders. At all the outlying stations they
> lived together with and in the manner of the natives, taking
> quite naturally to filth, privations and hardships, and on the
> other hand dividing with their savage friends all the little
> comforts of rude civilization which by chance fell to their
> lot.[19]

This quotation of Bancroft's is as much a reflection of nineteenth-
century America's preoccupation with the "white man's burden" as the term
"genocide" is a reflection of twentieth-century America's preoccupation
with what might be called the "white man's guilt complex." Neither is an
accurate depiction of the past.

A considerable amount of space has been devoted here to the period
of Russian trading activity in the Aleutians, an enterprise which continued, with more or less intensity in this portion of Alaska, until
Russia sold its American possessions to the United States in 1867.
The long consideration of this period is warranted, however, because of

---

18
William R. Hunt, Arctic Passage (New York: Charles Scribner's
Sons, 1975), p. 47.
19
Bancroft, History of Alaska, pp. 104, 383, 250-51.

the significance of that period in Aleut, as well as Russian and American,
history. Historians, on the other hand, have not always appeared to ap-
preciate that significance. In one of the more recent histories which
touches on Russian contact with the Aleutian Islands and their inhabitants the author used Steller's meeting with the Aleuts to emotionalize
for all he is worth:

> All the elements of the future subjugation of their eastern
> neighbors had passed in review. Tobacco and liquor had made
> their initial appearance. The first echoes of the firearms
> soon to enslave a free people resounded from the hills.[20]

Later, the same author curtly characterizes the fur trade's influence on
the Aleuts: "as a people they were debilitated and reduced to the status
of slaves."[21]

To insist on using trite, popular phraseology to describe the impact
of the fur trade on the Aleuts may endear an author to the more guilt-
laden segments of the reading public and scholarly community; it does little, however, to provide a better understanding of the wider implications
of that impact for the Aleuts. Such an understanding is an absolute necessity for an accurate history of that native group in Alaska.

Lantis, in her ethnohistoric study of the Aleuts during the early
Russian period, provides a beginning for a larger study of the fur trade's
impact and influence. She recognized that the major causes of Aleut
social change--physically, culturally, and psychologically--have their
roots in the nature of the fur trade as an institution, and in the day-

---

[20]
Hunt, _Arctic Passage_, p. 23.
[21]
. Ibid., p. 45.

to-day interaction of fur traders and Aleuts.

It is not enough to describe how the fur traders "enslaved" the Aleut population. More meaningful would be a discussion of how population loss, through Russian violence, disease, etc., changed aspects of Aleut life such as settlement patterns; or how the imposition of Russian-American Company regulation regarding the division of food for their native hunters affected division of labor in Aleut society, or how this affected subsistence patterns; how the Russians' utilization of Aleut men as hunters changed Aleut kinship relations, or the changes that thereby occurred in the Aleut family; how participation in the fur trade changed Aleut attitudes toward themselves and their relationship with their environment; how the relocation of major segments of the Aleut population changed all the socio-cultural and ecomomic systems which were based on generations of utilization of specific areas. The list of possibilities is almost endless, yet a real beginning has barely been made. Berreman has discussed some of the long-term results of forces set in motion by Russian contact with the Aleuts,[22] and the creole's place in the changing Aleut culture has recently begun to receive serious consideration.[23] And, of course, for the other side, a good administrative history of the Russian fur trade is needed, one that would take into account the Aleuts' influence on the changes that took place within that institution. Only through a study of this aspect of Russian-American history can the real

---

[22]
    Berreman, "Aleut Reference Group Alienation."
[23]
    Joan B. Townshend, "Mercantilism and Societal Change: An Ethnohistorical Examination of Some Essential Variables," Ethnohistory, 22(Winter, 1975):24.

nature of the Russian imperial advance in America be understood.

Closely allied to the fur trade as an institution, although at times strongly antagonistic to fur traders and Russian-American Company officials, was the Russian Orthodox Church and its attempts--and eventual success--in carrying Christianity to the Aleuts. Although Glotov baptized some Fox Island natives in 1759, the first Russian missionaries in Alaska were stationed at Kodiak in 1794. One of these, the Hieromonk Makarii, was sent to Unalaska. This missionary seems to have been quite successful. In a short time he had baptized most of the Island's Aleuts, although Veniaminov was later to find that they were Christian in name more than in fact. Makarii also seems to have taken the Aleuts' part against the fur traders, for in 1796 he and six Aleuts from Unalaska carried grievances against Shelikof's company back to Church superiors in Russia, who must have thought the missionary "a somewhat meddlesome ecclesiastic;" he was reprimanded "for absenting himself willfully from his appointed post of duty," and told to make further complaints "through the proper channel."[24]

The Russian-American Company's second charter, in 1821, required that the Company actively support missionary efforts in the Russian possessions, and to provide funds for establishing schools and churches. Within eight years five priests were sent to Alaska to take charge of the new missionary districts. Two of these were in the Aleutian Islands: in

---

[24]
Bancroft, History of Alaska, p. 364; Michael G. Kovach, "The Russian Orthodox Church in Russian America". unpublished doctoral dissertation, University of Pittsburgh, 1957, p. 276.

1824 Veniaminov was appointed to the Unalaska District, which included the Fox and Pribilof Islands; Jacob Netzvetov was assigned to the Atka District, which included the Andreanof, Rat, Near, and Commander Islands groups, as well as the Kurile Islands. Veniaminov, who established a school on Unalaska in 1825 and built a church on the island the following year, remained at this post for ten years, after which he went to Sitka as Bishop. Netzvetov remained on Atka until 1840, when he was reassigned to western Alaska.[25]

Although the bare outlines of Russian missionary activity are known, most discussions of the Russian Church in Alaska center around Veniaminov. His success in translating the Church's liturgy into Aleut, and developing an Aleut reader for use in native schools are readily acknowledged, but these discussions follow Veniaminov to Sitka, leaving missionary work in the Aleutians relatively untouched for the remainder of the Russian period. Portions of Netzvetov's journals have been translated in the multivolume Documents Relative to the History of Alaska, however, and historians should be able to locate his complete journals, as well as those of other priests, in order to provide a broader view of missionary work in the Aleutian Islands.

The Russian Orthodox Church's activities in the Aleutians are not only significant in terms of the history of a major Russian institution in North America, but also in relation to Aleut culture change. As noted earlier, Lantis remarked on the Russian Church's effect of lessening

---

25
Ibid., p. 140; Basil M. Bensin, Russian Orthodox Church in Alaska, 1794-1967 (Sitka: Russian Orthodox Greek Catholic Church of North America, Diocese of Alaska, 1968), p. 36.

Aleut dependence and confidence in their own religious practices, and the Aleuts came more and more to rely on the Russian Church not only in spiritual matters, but also for health services and education.

Present-day Aleut feeling for the Russian Orthodox Church indicate how successful its initial efforts have turned out to be. In May, 1975 _Alaska_ Magazine printed a letter from an Assembly of God minister who claimed that the Russian Church on one of the Pribilof Islands had almost driven him off the Island, and that the Church was therefore unmindful of the American tradition of freedom of religion. Two months later, _Alaska_ carried a letter from the Island's Community Council, which declared the "solid foundation of Christian faith" of the Pribilof Islanders. "During the hard years of dictatorial rule under the Russian flag," said the Council, "and continuing under the American flag, the Orthodox Church gave them their only hope for freedom. And now, nearly 200 years later, the ugliest of hardships are gone; the Church has proved its strength." To demonstrate how ingrained their religion has become, the Council closed its letter by describing the Russian Church as the peoples' "old and sacred way of worship."[26]

When discussions of the Aleutian Islands in terms of their history appear, two thoughts generally spring into the minds of historians and their readers: the Russian fur trade (sometimes accompanied by the more subtle thought of Russian Orthodox missionary activity), and World War II (considered hardly at all from the Native standpoint). Yet in the almost eighty years between the end of Russian activity in the Aleutians

---

[26] _Alaska_, 41(May, 1975):23; _Alaska_, 41(July, 1975):13.

and the beginning of Japanese control of the western Islands there were highly significant events and processes taking place. More importantly, the sources for interpreting these events and processes exist, although they have hardly been utilized.

A few examples of the Aleutian historical topics which might prove provocative for future study will suffice. Following the American purchase of Alaska the Russian-American Company's trade was taken over by the Alaska Commercial Company. An adequate study of this Company's activities in the Aleutians is still lacking.

Perhaps even more interesting would be a study of American education and other social services extended to the Aleuts, and their effect on the Native inhabitants. Unalaska was one of the initial testing grounds for Sheldon Jackson's monumental project of introducing reindeer into Alaska to aid the Natives. And as part of Jackson's education and mission programs Methodist missionaries arrived on Unalaska in 1896. When the Bureau of Indian Affairs took over the education of Alaska's Natives in 1931, only three schools existed in the Aleutians; within ten years five or more had been established, and according to the reports that are available, education was only one of the functions of the teachers at these schools.

Also in terms of government interest in providing services to the Aleutian Islands, the Revenue Marine Service, later the Coast Guard, visited the Islands periodically beginning in the late nineteenth century to provide medical aid and guard against the illegal liquor traffic. The reports of these visits provide valuable information about Aleut life in the nineteenth and early twentieth centuries.

In order to fully understand the changes in Aleut life style and culture after the end of the Russian period, economic history must also be considered. By the time Ivan Petroff made his report for the 1880 census, the most valuable sea otter hunting areas had shifted to the eastern Aleutians, particularly the Sanak group; there were trade rivalries at Unga; the cod-fishing industry was doing an enormous business off the Popof Islands south of the Alaska Peninsula. Petroff also mentioned the rise of fox farming in the western and middle Aleutians after the Russian-American Company left, the development and disappointment of the coal mines on Unga Island, and the Russian agricultural colony which had been established on Korovinsky--they were not allowed to hunt, but instead grew potatoes and turnips, and kept a small herd of cattle--which, since the departure of the Russians, had taken up fur hunting again. Perhaps Petroff's most cogent remark was on the state of Aleut society at the end of the nineteenth century: their "individuality as a race or tribe has almost completely disappeared."[27] This was a common observation made about many native groups in the United States at this period; that the Aleuts did survive, despite relative isolation and continuing decline in numbers due to disease, would seem to provoke historical inquiry as to why they remain. No historian, however, seems willing to take up the task.

These are but a few of the factors to be considered in a well-rounded history of the Aleutian Islands between 1867 and 1942. There are many others. Perhaps one more should be mentioned--there is absolutely no study of the beginnings of American interaction with the Aleuts, or a

---

[27] Ivan Petroff, "Report on the Population, Industries, and Resources of Alaska," United States Census Office, 10th Census, 1880 (Washington, D.C.: Government Printing Office, 1884), p. 18.

comparison of this with earlier Russian interethnic relations in this region.

World War II in the Aleutians has received relatively good historical treatment.[28] The story of Aleuts in the war, however, and the war's long-term effect on the Aleuts, have not been considered in these studies. Yet in World War II the Aleuts underwent a major relocation which exceeded even the relocations under the Russian-American Company. The changes in Aleut life and society brought about by this twentieth-century relocation are only beginning to be studied and understood.

When the Japanese bombed Dutch Harbor, on Unalaska Island, in June, 1942 and then turned west to occupy Kiska and Attu in the western Aleutians, there were forty-five Aleuts and two white teachers on the latter island. The Japanese attacked Attu on June 7, killing the white schoolteacher, Charles Foster Jones, the island's only casualty. Mrs. Jones was taken almost immediately to Japan, where she was imprisoned outside Yokohama for the rest of the war, being released by American occupation troops in September, 1945.

The forty-five Aleuts of Attu remained on the island with their Japanese captors for three months, after which time they too were taken to Japan as prisoners of war. In Otaru, on the island of Hokkaido, they

---

28

Particularly two works: Brian Garfield, The Thousand-Mile War; World War II in Alaska and the Aleutians (New York: Doubleday & Company, Inc., 1969); Samuel Eliot Morison, History of United States Naval Operations in World War II, Vol. 4, Coral Sea, Midway, and Submarine Actions, May 1942-August, 1942 (Boston: Little, Brown & Co., 1949), which discusses the Japanese invasion of the western Aleutians, and Vol. 7, Aleutians, Gilberts and Marshalls, June 1942-April 1944 (Boston: Little, Brown & Co., 1951), which discusses the American reoccupation of Attu and Kiska.

were given housing rented from the government of the city, and were guarded by civilian police. The Aleut men were put to work digging clay, while some of the women did hospital janitorial work. Due to poor rations, and probably poor living conditions, many of the Aleuts contracted tuberculosis and died. Of the forty-five who went to Japan, only twenty-four Aleuts were still alive when they were discovered by American troops in October, 1945. They were returned to the United States, where it was decided that because there were too few of them to comprise a viable village community, and because it would be too expensive for the government to rebuild the Attu village for such a small number, these repatriated Aleuts would join the villagers of Atka Island, halfway along the Aleutian Chain. Sixteen of the former Attu Aleuts arrived on Atka in December, 1945.

Soon after the Japanese attack on Dutch Harbor and the occupation of the western Aleutians, the Aleuts of other islands in the Chain, as well as the population of the Pribilofs, were removed by the United States government and relocated at various points in southeast Alaska until the Japanese threat to the security of the islands was removed. Many of these relocated Aleuts died also, due to diseases contracted and deprivations suffered in their new, unfamiliar environment.

The end of the war and the return of the Aleuts to their islands did not mean a return to the way of life they had known prior to their relocation. Aleut villages and personal possessions had been destroyed, and had to be rebuilt or replaced by the government. Part of the economic security the Aleuts had had from hunting, trapping, and fishing before the war was lost due to a collapse in the fox-trapping industry. Aleuts in some areas grew dependent on Aleutian military bases for work opportunities and social services. Many Aleuts were drawn away from their islands to other areas of Alaska to find work, particularly in crab fishing and processing; this has undoubtedly caused changes in community and family structure such as were caused by hunters going off for long periods under the Russian fur traders.

Greater contact with American whites--carrying American values--both on an individual basis and through government agencies, has also been influential in changing the Aleut way of life in the twentieth century. Schoolteachers, health officials, and other social service agents provide only a portion of the influences which such increased contact has on Aleut society. Storeowners in the Aleutian villages have often had a great effect on the economic life of the communities, not the least of which is as outlets for an increased cash income.[29]

Increased Bureau of Indian Affairs programs have also been influential; some of the Aleut villages incorporated under the Indian Reorganization Act in the late 1930s. Sometimes this incorporation has had good results in the village, while at other times, such as in the village of Nikolski on Umnak Island, it resulted in factionalism in the community over lines of authority.[30]

The enactment of the Alaska Native Land Claims Act in 1971, with incorporated villages (13 in the Aleutian region) and the larger, profit oriented Aleut Regional Corporation, will certainly cause far-reaching

---

[29]
Berreman, "Inquiry into Community Integration in an Aleutian Village," American Anthropologist, 57 (February, 1955): 52.
[30]
Ibid., p. 53.

changes in all aspects of Aleut life and culture. But only an investigation of where the Aleuts have been, and all the changes they have undergone, can provide the basis for an understanding of changes which will occur in the future.

The history of any group of people, when looked at over a long period of that group's life, is the story of culture change. This is especially true when one group's culture is engulfed by another. The Aleutian Islands provide a stage for an incredible story of such change over a period of more than 200 years; up to the present time, however, only small portions of that story have been told with any degree of detail and interpretation. It has been noted that the period of Russian contact has been studied in some detail, and its story retold by numerous historians, beginning while the fur trade was still in its infancy. The later periods of Aleut history have not been studied as closely; yet these later periods, in terms of their effect on Aleut culture, are of great significance. One anthropologist has noted that because of Russian participation in the Aleut culture, and the Russianization of Aleut life due in large part to the influence of the Russian Orthodox Church,

> nondisruptive, selective assimilation of the new traits was
> . . . effectively facilitated. . . . Furthermore, Russian con-
> tacts decreased in intensity with time. As a result, although
> hardship and conflict were prominent, and in spite of the ac-
> quisition of a good many Russian tools, techniques, and foods,
> as well as religion, Aleut ways were to a remarkable extent
> preserved. Interests and goals remained attainable within the
> village, and in time adjustments were made to the Russian
> influences.[31]

In the American period, he continues, "contacts have become increasingly

---

[31]
Ibid., p. 51.

intense and demanding, giving the Aleuts progressively less chance for selective acceptance and gradual adjustment."[32] A complete, detailed, and interpretive history of the Aleuts would do much in the way of explaining culture change in Alaska, as well as provide an interesting example of contact, conflict, and change to compare with other areas of the United States where such processes occurred.

The sources are available for such a study, either of the Aleutian region as a whole, or--and this would be less desirable in the long run, but perhaps useful as a beginning--of a particular portion of the Aleutians. Perhaps the most naturally specific area which deserves a good interpretive history is the Pribilof group. Uninhabited at the time of their discovery by the Russians in 1786, they were quickly occupied by Russian fur hunters, who colonized Aleuts from other islands onto St. Paul and St. George. The intensity of Russian fur seal exploitation on these islands had depleted the fur seal herds by almost ninety percent in the twenty years after their discovery, and Nikolai Rezanov, an official of the Russian government visiting the area in 1805, put a halt to the killing of seals for a period until the herds could regain their numbers. Later, under the Russian-American Company, alternate hunting grounds were established in order to preserve the herds.[33] And, of course, during the Russian period Russian Orthodox missionaries had contacts with the Aleuts of the Pribilofs--the islands were part of the Unalaska mission district-- and churches were built on St. Paul in 1819 and on St. George in 1833.

---

[32]
    Ibid., p. 55.
[33]
    Bancroft, History of Alaska, pp. 446, 582.

After the American purchase of Alaska, troops had to be stationed in the Pribilofs to stop the intense rivalry among fur companies for the lucrative fur seals. The Treasury Department finally received control of the fur rookeries, and leased the islands to the Alaska Commercial Company. Treasury agents were stationed on the islands from 1870 to supervise the taking of seals. In the late nineteenth century the Pribilofs became the focus of international attention over the pelagic sealing question.

In 1942 the Aleuts living on the Pribilofs, as on other islands, were removed to southeast Alaska because of the Japanese threat in the Pacific. When the islanders returned in 1945 they faced the same problems of rebuilding their villages and their social and economic well-being as did other Aleuts. Today, the two villages of St. George and St. Paul are incorporated under the Alaska Native Claims Settlement Act.

As can be seen, the history of the Pribilof Islands provides an almost microcosmic view of the history of the Aleuts. Of course, there are major differences between the history of the Pribilof Islands and the history of Aleutian Islands groups--the Pribilofs were uninhabited at the time of white contact, and their settlement was an explicit act of colonization of Aleuts to exploit the fur resources of the islands. This in itself poses interesting questions for a study of culture change in these islands. But the Pribilofs can also serve as a focus for studies of conservation in the Aleutians, comparative administration (Russian and American) by government and fur companies, religious history, international relations, World War II and its effects, etc.

Sources are readily available for a study of the Pribilofs. Not only are there records of the Russian-American Company and Russian Orthodox missionaries, but there are also Treasury Department reports and the

Pribilof Island logbooks kept by Treasury agents on St. Paul and St. George. These latter sources provide descriptions of day-by-day activities on the Pribilofs--seal harvests; departure and arrival of vessels; information on fox trapping; marriage, birth, and death records; building improvements; medical services; and school attendance--from 1870 to 1961. One of the more significant sections of these logbooks concerns the Pribilof Islanders' relocation to southeast Alaska during World War II.

This discussion of the Pribilof Islands is just an indication of what needs to be done in Aleutian history. And a full history of the Aleutians must be written, not only to provide Alaskans or Alaskan Natives with a working knowledge of their past, but also to provide an understanding of processes that took place on many frontiers of North America. And if culture change is one of the major themes which should be studied in relation to Aleut history, then a comparative look at this and other American frontiers is another theme which requires more adequate discussion.

Comparing Alaska in general, or the Aleutian Islands in particular, to other frontier areas of America can be fruitful as well as interesting. There are many differences between the Alaska frontier and the frontiers of the Lower 48, but there are similarities as well, similarities which can help clarify the nature of interethnic contact and the cultural processes involved in and initiated by such contact. Perhaps a comparison between Russian exploration, exploitation, and missionary activities in the Aleutians and similar Spanish activities in the American Southwest will clarify European methods and attitudes toward colonization and Native groups in the New World. Certainly many aspects of these methods and attitudes still survive today, both in the Aleutians and in the Southwest. And perhaps if historians study the Black Legend which was directed against Spain--in part because of that country's actions in the New World--a different perspective of the same sort of legend which has developed around Russian activities in the Aleutians and elsewhere in Alaska might be attained.

A similar comparative study could be made in the area of United States Indian policy. In order to understand the development of the Alaska Native Claims Settlement Act one must first understand the development of American Indian policies in Alaska and in the Lower 48. A part of those policies involve the Aleutian Islands and their inhabitants.

Today there are over 3,000 Aleuts enrolled as stockholders in the Aleut Corporation, and thirteen village corporations spread from the Alaska Peninsula to Atka and the Pribilof Islands with a total population of almost 2,500. This is a considerable decline from the population of between 12,000 and 15,000, and the hundreds of small settlements that are known to have been scattered throughout the 1,100-mile Aleutian Chain at the time of initial Russian contact nearly 250 years ago. The Aleuts have been relocated perhaps earlier, more often, and more recently than any other North American Native group. Their religion has changed, their economy modified numerous times, and their culture disrupted. Their continued existence, however, shows a resilient and adaptive nature to their culture and their environment. Their history is important to themselves, to their neighbors among Alaskans--both Native and white--and to the nation as a whole. The interpretation of that history has too often been neglected for the sake of platitudes and generalities. With all their past hardships, and the promise of continued change in the future, the Aleuts deserve better of modern scholars.

V. GENERAL DESCRIPTION AND SIGNIFICANCE OF ALEUT HISTORIC SITES

Section 14(h)(1) of the Alaska Native Claims Settlement Act of 1971 (ANCSA) allows each Native Regional Corporation to select a portion of two million allotted acres as historic and cemetery sites. The regional corporations will obtain surface rights only to these sites, and according to the rules and regulations for this section of ANCSA the corporations must maintain these sites in a manner so as not to impair their historic integrity. Applications for site selections were required to include a statement of significance justifying each site's selection as an historic place (cemetery sites did not require such justification). The criteria for justifying the historic qualities of a site were similar to the criteria developed for nominating sites to the National Register: association with prominent events and people in the region's history; symbolic cultural values; characteristic design or construction; and past or potential yield of archaeological evidence.

By June 30, 1976 the Aleut Corporation filed applications for the selection of 411 historic sites. These selections equalled 4,453 acres, broken down by Island group as follows:

Near	612.5	acres
Rat	927	"
Andreanof	1,788.5	"
Four Mountains	186	"
Fox	449	"
Sanak	10	"

Alaska Peninsula	313	acres
Shumagin & Popof	167	"
Total	4,453	(10.83 average site size)

Due to differences within the Aleutian region--and the diverse intensities of previous site surveys in many areas of the Aleutians--the sites vary considerably in nature. The largest number of sites selected by the Corporation are on Amchitka (77 sites, with a total of 732 acres) and Adak (76 sites, total of 725 acres) Islands. On the other end of the range are the small, rocky islets of Ship Rock and Pustoi Island, both in Umnak Pass between Umnak and Unalaska Islands, which are each barely 500 yards across; Ship Rock is the site of two important burial caves studied by Hrdlicka in the 1930s, while an old Aleut settlement site is located on Pustoi.

The largest single site selected by the Corporation (150 acres) is the area formerly comprising Attu village on Chichagof Harbor on the northeastern coast of Attu Island. This village was occupied until its inhabitants were removed to Japan as prisoners of war following the Japanese invasion of the western Aleutians in 1942. The village itself was destroyed by American bombing raids against Japanese positions and later military construction. Again, on the other end of the scale sites as small as five or six acres were selected on many islands throughout the Chain and on the Alaska Peninsula.

It would probably be unwarrantable even to hazard a guess as to the relative number of selected historic sites which fall into the general categories of prehistoric (pre-contact), historic (post-contact), and protohistoric. As has been mentioned previously, many of the islands became uninhabited early in the Russian period, and many settlement sites were probably also abandoned for one reason or another before contact between the Aleuts and the Russians.

Historic documentation of early contact in the Aleutians is not as adequate as it could be in helping to determine which sites were occupied when the islands were first visited by the Russians. These accounts generally note which islands, or which portions of the coasts of specific islands were visited, but are notoriously lacking in explicit information on the location of all but the largest Aleut settlements. This is not surprising, considering the drifting, seasonal nature of settlement patterns in relation to the availability of subsistence resources. By the end of the period of Russian contact, most of the Aleutian Islands--including the islands between Attu and Atka, where a great number of selected sites are located (257 sites; 2,495.5 acres)--were completely devoid of occupied Aleut settlements. This area was, however, often visited seasonally by Aleut hunters, and Kanaga was utilized for fox farming in the early twentieth century.[1]

Some sites, or areas in which sites were later found by surveys, are familiar to present-day Aleut hunters who utilize some of the islands fur subsistence purposes, or who trapped furs on the islands. Bergsland, in his discussion of Aleut place names, notes that some of these areas are named for the subsistence resources available there, or subsistence-related activities pursued at the site; this indicates traditional use,

---

[1] Lynda Sekora, "A Visit to Kanaga Island," Alaska, 38(November, 1972):24. Other areas were also utilized for fox farming; see George L. DeVenne, "Blue Gold of the Aleutians," Alaska Sportsman, 5 (July, 1939): 8-9, 22-24.

and traditional memory of, the area (See, for example, site AT-3 on Atka Island, the name of which is translated as "'sitting together,' an ancient village site and a place where trappers used to sojourn"[2]).

Other sites are still important in traditional oral histories of the Aleut population, although the areas in which these sites are located have been unoccupied, or even unvisited, for a long time (see site TK-1, on Tagalak Island, which is remembered as an area of inter-island warfare; and site KN-28, on Kanaga Island, which has spiritual and symbolic significance).

Some general characteristics can be noted for the sites selected by the Aleut Corporation. Many areas in which these sites are located are typical of the topographic areas noted for Aleut settlement sites--coves, isthmuses between two bodies of water, narrow points of land, etc. Differentiation of these sites into base settlements and seasonal camps will probably require at least superficial archaeological testing, if not even more extensive investigation. Some work along these lines was done during the Amchitka survey in 1969-1970, and some of the sites on that island were identified as probable staging areas for hunting and fishing and as sites for manufacturing tools; these activities seem to have been distinctive of the beach-terrace middens tested during the survey. Sites located on bluffs above the beaches offered good observation points from which to spot migrating game and enemies, and they provided good protection from storms as well. The work on Amchitka was only a beginning, however, and merely an indication of the work that has yet to be done in this and other

------

[2]
Bergsland, "Aleut Dialects," p. 34.

portions of the Aleutian Islands.

In terms of the statements of significance filed with each site application, and the criteria used to justify the site's selection as an historic site, a few words will suffice. Most of the sites were archaeological sites which have yielded important information about Aleut history and prehistory, or, as in the majority of cases, have the potential of yielding such information. Such information is particularly important for the better delineation of Aleut settlement patterns, subsistence utilization, population migrations, and regional diversities in these and other aspects of Aleut life and culture.

Other sites--such as sites on Kirilof Bay on Amchitka, which was inhabited until 1849--have historic meaning which is important not only specifically for the Native population of the Aleutians, but which are also significant to the understanding of European contact and influences in this portion of the New World. Most of the historic sites--the larger settlements which were established by the Russian American Company and which into and through the American period--are generally located in areas which have been selected by the various village corporations.

One historic trail or portage has been definitely determined, linking two sites (AD-18 and AD-19) located on two bays one mile apart on the western coast of Adak Island. Hrdlicka, who investigated in this area in the 1930s, was told by his Aleut informant that one of these sites (AD-18) was a large settlement, while the other (AD-19) was utilized only in the summer, probably as a subsistence camp. Similar portages are undoubtedly common in other areas of this and other Aleutian Islands, used for both flight from enemies and trails between seasonal camps and more permanent settlements.

Burial caves selected by the Corporation, when a nearby settlement site was not involved, were also selected as historic sites rather than cemetery sites. Far from being merely an area for burying Aleut dead, such caves are also significant in the feelings and associations held by the Aleut population, as well as having provided important data on aspects of Aleut culture.

Historic sites selected on the Alaska Peninsula have generally the same significance as other sites in the Aleutian region; they are archaeological sites which have the potential of yielding information for delineating Aleut prehistory and history. As it seems that most sites in this area were used only seasonally, future investigations here could help clarify Aleut subsistence utilization in the area. Moreover, the Alaska Peninsula is an important area for the study of Aleut migration into the Aleutian Islands. It is also a region of cultural contact--warfare, trade, and cultural diffusion--between Aleuts and other Natives of southwestern Alaska. Some of the Alaska Peninsula sites are also important in post-contact Aleutian history. Site PN-T was an historic settlement connected with mining explorations on the Alaska Peninsula, and PN-R is the site of a former cannery; both are significant in terms of delineating the economic history of the area and its inhabitants.

Sites in the Shumagin Islands and other islands off the southern coast of the Alaska Peninsula have similar qualities of significance to the Peninsula sites: they have the potential of yielding information delineating Aleut migration into the Aleutians, cultural diffusion between Aleuts and other Alaskan Natives, and details of changing economic patterns in the area over a long period of time.

When possible in the statements of significance, information on specific sites in the Aleutians and Alaska Peninsula was combined with information on the history of the island, island group, or portion of the Peninsula with which the sites are associated. This was done to give a broader perspective and background to the qualities of significance inherent in each site.

VI. RECOMMENDATIONS

Recommendations for the management of Aleutian cultural resources fall into three categories: the development of adequate Aleut histories, the management of cultural properties by the Aleut Corporation, and the nomination of these properties to the National Register.

At the present time the status of historical writing concerning the Aleutian Islands, their inhabitants, and the historical processes influencing them can be characterized as haphazard. Specific time periods and topics within these periods (fur trade, World War II) have been more or less fully treated, at least in a narrative, if not interpretive, sense. Also, Lantis has produced a starting point for an ethnohistorical study of Aleut culture, and that culture's response to outside influences; this too has focussed on the early years of Russian activity in the Aleutians.

In future histories of the Aleutian region, work that has already been done must be integrated with new data to form a more complete picture of changes in Aleut culture throughout time, as well as the effects which the Aleutian environment and the native Aleuts had on the non-Native population which came to the area. Specific themes, especially those related to various aspects of culture change, must be addressed in these histories. The Aleutian region seems to be ideally suited for an ethnohistorical study along the lines of Dorothy Jean Ray's Eskimo of Bering Strait. Such a study could easily be a multivolume work, due to the length of time in which interethnic contact occurred in the Aleutians, as well as because of the varied methods, goals, and results of that contact. A shorter, general history of the region might also be valuable, but such an overview should only be a prelude to more sophisticated, in-depth treatments.

Although concerns other than culture histories are more pressing for the Aleut Corporation and the thirteen village corporations within the region at the present time, encouragement should be given to interested historians--Aleuts as well as whites--to begin to lay the foundation for full historical treatments of the areas. Aleut historians, especially, could begin by writing histories which reflect the "Native point of view." The Aleuts themselves are in the best position to provide and explain their own oral histories, folklore, and even Native biographies. Studies of this nature, too, like general historical overviews of the region, will provide portions of the more sophisticated ethnohistories of the region which will eventually be written.

The scattered archaeological information must also be gathered and integrated before the writing of adequate Aleut ethnohistories can be successfully attempted. The ill-defined nature of, and regional (inter-island and intra-island) diversities in, settlement patterns, subsistence utilization, population size, migrations, and other aspects of Aleut life must be clarified, especially for the pre-contact and early contact periods. It would be advantageous to archaeologists, cultural anthropologists, and historians if more complete surveys and testing were conducted in areas of the Aleutians which have hitherto received relatively little attention. The Aleuts would also gain from such investigation, at least in terms of better inventories of their cultural resources.

Management of the cultural resources (Aleut historic sites) which are already known and which may yet be found in the Aleutian Islands and on the Alaska Peninsula must be linked with their interpretation and cautious exploitation of their potential for yielding information which will add to the knowledge of human occupation of these areas. The major problem seems to be that the management of these historic sites is not a high priority for either the Aleut Corporation or the Aleut League at the present time. Moreover, as the major portion of the Aleutian Chain is a wildlife refuge, the majority of historic sites selected under Section 14(h)(1) of ANCSA are therefore felt to be adequately protected, aside from the restrictive covenants which will be attached to the sites which will eventually be owned by the Aleut Corporation. There is also little fear on the part of the Corporation's Land Department that pot-hunting is a major threat to the sites. Difficulty of access to the sites is certainly a deterrent to intensive pot-hunting. Information on such activities in areas such as the Adak Naval base, which has many nearby Aleut sites, and other areas of military operations is unavailable.

Because of the above factors, the protective aspects of the National Register are seen as unnecessary additions, and little or no consideration has as yet been given to the possibility of nominating any of the sites selected to the Register. Furthermore, there is the possibility of an arrangement between the Fish and Wildlife Service and the Aleut Corporation whereby the former will agree to manage the sites and maintain their historic integrity if the Corporation decides not to undertake their actual ownership. If such an arrangement is made, it is likely that the Corporation will accept title to only a relatively small number of the more significant sites.

Nomination to the National Register of historic sites not in the wildlife refuge, and particularly those sites which are within village and regional selections, would probably be advantageous. Such nominations, however, should be initiated by the village corporations concerned. Care should be taken not to rush in and nominate all sites in the region; it is likely that many site nominations would be rejected, which would cause dissatisfaction and even more cautious action in the future on the part of the village and regional corporations. When possible, in dealing with archaeological sites, nomination of archaeological districts should be encouraged, rather than the nomination of single sites.

Aleutian sites already on the National Register are: the Anangula archaeological district, the oldest coastal site known for Beringia; the Chaluka archaeological site, which had provided significant information on Aleut life during its 4,000 years of occupation; the Church of the Holy Assension, on Unalaska, which was built by Veniaminov in 1826; and the Fur Seal Rookeries on St. Paul Island. All of these sites are located within village selections, and all, moreover, are National Landmarks. Also proposed for Landmark status are: the Attu battlefield, which is historically as well as archaeologically significant; the Port Moller Hot Springs archaeological site, significant in contributing information on cultural diffusion through the Alaska Peninsula; and the Sitka Spruce Plantation on Amaknak Island northeast of Unalaska village, which was planted by the Russians in 1805. Attu village and the Port Moller Hot Springs site have both been selected by the Aleut Corporation under Section 14(h)(1) of ANCSA. Amaknak Island is part of the Unalaska village selection.

These are the types of sites which should probably receive priority in nomination to the National Register. There are many more like them in

74

the Aleutians (perhaps something along the lines of an "Amchitka Archaeological and Historic District"). In any case, such nominations would require further surveying, testing, and historical documentation.

Finally, although somewhat out of context, a statement must be made concerning the proposed Aleutian Islands cleanup project proposed by Congress, to be carried out by the Army Corps of Engineers. This project involves the removal from the region of the debris which was left by military construction during and after World War II, and the restoration of as much of the affected area as possible to its "natural" condition prior to that construction. Twenty-eight sites of former military construction have been identified by the Corps of Engineers, from Port Heiden on the Alaska Peninsula to Attu Island. The military refuse poses a threat to safety in areas presently inhabited, and pollution problems thorughout the region.

A recently-completed study[1] of the problem notes four alternative degrees of debris removal and disposal--total cleanup (restoration of the area to pre-World War II conditions), alternate cleanup (removal of 90% of the total debris), minimum cleanup (removal of only safety and pollution hazards), and no action at all. The cost for total cleanup is estimated as $117,000,000., that for alternate cleanup $79,000,000., and that for minimum cleanup $22,000,000. The alternate cleanup plan seems to be the most realistic of the Corps' proposals.

It will probably be years before proposals made by the Corps of Engineers will be approved and funds fully appropriated for the project.

---

[1] U.S. Army, Corps of Engineers, Alaska District, Debris Removal and Cleanup Study, Aleutian Islands and Lower Alaska Peninsula, Alaska, sections contributed by Thomas Dowell, Jr. Anchorage: June, 1977.

The National Park Service and the Aleut Corporation should keep up with the proposals and eventual implementation of the project in order to mitigate any adverse effects the cleanup would have on the cultural resources in the area. As a rough estimate, at least 100 known historic and archaeological sites in the Aleutian Islands are located in the proposed cleanup areas; this does not include the number of sites in proposed cleanup areas on the Alaska Peninsula. Military construction has already damaged many Aleut settlement sites. Removing the debris could further endanger these and other types of sites. In addition, some of the miltiary construction in areas such as--but not restricted to--Attu, Amchitka, Kiska, and Umnak is an integral part of Aleutian history. Historians and archaeologists must, therefore, be included in any attempted cleanup operations throughout the Aleutian Islands and on the lower Alaska Peninsula.

The report submitted by the Corps of Engineers recognizes the necessity for including historians and archaeologists on the cleanup investigation teams, yet without continued National Park Service and Aleut Corporation input as the project develops, anthropological and historic aspects of the project may be inadequately carried out.

BIBLIOGRAPHY

An annotated bibliography of the Aleutian region has already been
published: Dorothy M. Jones and John R. Wood, An Aleut Bibliography
(Fairbanks: University of Alaska, Institute of Social, Economic and
Government Research, 1975). This bibliography is divided into four major
sections: 1). alphabetical list of literature by author; 2). complete
bibliographic information for each source and annotation; 3). list of
literature organized by period of observation, i.e., precontact, Russian,
American, and contemporary; 4). list according to subject, i.e. explorers'
accounts, history, anthropology, archaeology, economics. Jones and Wood
annotate 354 works, and there is an appendix with seven annotated biblio-
graphical works.

This bibliography is only an indication of the amount of research
that has been done on Aleut history, society, and culture. In the following pages I will provide a bibliography of works more recent than, or
overlooked by, Jones and Wood. There will follow a description of scme
of the more important archival sources for the Aleutians.

Aigner, Jean S. "Carved and Incised Stones from Chaluka and Anangula." Anthropological Papers of the University of Alaska, 15(No. 2, 1972): 39-51.

Discusses material and motifs of stones found at these two important archaeological sites on Nikolski Bay, Umnak Island.

_____. "The Unifacial, Core and Blade Site on Anangula Island, Aleutians." Arctic Anthropology, 7(No. 2, 1970): 59-88.

Detailed description of the work done at Anangula, and the artifacts recovered there. Important source for Aleut prehistory.

Alaska, State of. Alaska Regional Profiles; Southwest Region. Edited by Lidia L. Selkregg. Published by University of Alaska, Arctic Environmental Information and Data Center, n.d.).

Narrative description, maps, tables, photographs of Aleutian climate, topography, flora and fauna, land use, and brief dicussion of history of inhabitants. Excellent background study prepared for Joint Federal-State Land Use Planning Commission for Alaska. Also covers Kuskokwim Bay and Bristol Bay subregions.

"The Aleutian Islands--Alaska's Beautiful 'Junkyard.'" Alaska, (March, 1977):52-53.

Two pages of color photographs of World War II debris left on Aleutians.

"American Forces in the Aleutians." Military Engineer, 33(July, 1943): 347-51.

U.S. Navy photographs of American servicemen, shore line and terrain of Aleutian Islands.

Andreev, A.I. Russian Discoveries in the Pacific and in North America in the Eighteenth and Nineteenth Centuries. Translated by Carl Ginsburg for the American Council of Learned Societies. Ann Arbor: Edwards Bros., 1944.

Discovery of Umnak, Unalaska, and the Andreanof Islands; description of Shelikov's activities; journal of Lisianski's round-the-world voyage.

Andrews, Clarence L. "Children of the Sea." Alaska Sportsman, 4(July, 1938):8-9, 27-28, 31-32.

Discusses the importance of the sea otter in Russian trade. Trading activities in the Aleutians from Russian times to the early twentieth century.

_____. "Marine Disasters of the Alaska Route." Pacific Northwest Quarterly, 7(January, 1916):21-37.

Concentrates on southeast Alaska, but also has listing of wrecks,
some of them in the Aleutians, especially in eastern Aleutians
and Shumagins. Good indication of amount of shipping in area.

_____. "The War in Alaska." Alaska Life, 5(November, 1942):5-8.

Popular description of invasion of Aleutians by Japanese earlier in
the year; discusses significance of Aleutians in strategy of the war.
Gives good idea of popular thought about Aleutian invasion.

Ashbrook, Frank G. "Blue Fox Farming in Alaska." U.S. Dept. of Agricul-
ture, Bulletin No. 1350. Washington, D.C. Government Printing
Office, 1925.

History of Blue Fox farming and details on some areas in the Aleutians
suited for fox farming.

"The Battle of the Aleutians." Alaska Call, 1 (September, 1959):4-5, 23.

Brief overview of Aleutian campaign from Japanese attack on Dutch
Harbor to the occupation of Kiska.

Bean, Tarleton H. "The Fishery Resources and Fishing Grounds of Alaska,"
in Goode, G.B., et. al., The Fisheries and Fishery Industries of
the U.S. Prepared through the cooperation of the Commissioner of
Fisheries and the Superintendent of the Tenth Census. 8 vols.
Washington, D.C.: Government Printing Office, 1884-1887.

Description of fishing grounds by district, including Shumagin
Islands, Unalaska, Pribilofs. Lists of settlements, etc.

Beech, Mary L. "refugees from the Pribilofs." Alaska Life, 7(August,
1944):18-21.

Discussion of Pribilof Aleuts relocated in southeast Alaska.

Berkh, Vasilii N. A Chronological History of the Discovery of the Aleutian Islands, or the Exploits of Russian Merchants, With the Supplement of Historical Data on the Fur Trade. Translated by Dmitri
Krenov, edited by Richard A. Pierce. Kingston, Ontario: Limestone
Press, 1974.

Title is self-explanatory. One of the most important sources used
by Bancroft for the early trading voyages to the Aleutians.

Brice, Howard. "Etta Jones . . . P.O.W." Alaska Life, 8(December,
1945):48-51.

Probably the best account of the invasion of the Island of Attu by
the Japanese in June, 1942 and Mrs. Jones' imprisonment in Japan.

_____. "Men from St. Paul." Alaska Life, 7(September, 1944): 30-31.

Photographs of American troops stationed on St. Paul Island in Pribilofs during World War II.

Brooks, Charles Wolcott. "Report of Japanese Vessels Wrecked in the North Pacific Ocean, from the Earliest Records to the Present Time." California Academy of Sciences, Proceedings, 5(1975):50-66.

Location and condition of sixty Japanese wrecks, including some in Aleutian Islands.

Bruce, Davis, and Court, Arnold. "Trees for the Aleutians." Geographical Review, 35(July, 1945):418-23.

Account of the planting of trees in Aleutians by military in World War II. Also has description of Aleutian environment.

Butler, Ralph E. "Monster Mammals of the Aleutian Seas." Alaska Sportsman, 11(April, 1945):8-9, 33-41; (May, 1945):12-13, 25-31.

Good discussion of whaling activities based at Akutan in the eastern Aleutians in the 1920s. Photographs.

Butts, Rose Curtice. "Prisoners from Alaska." Alaska Sportsman, 14 (May, 1948):14-15, 36-39.

Author was a teacher at Eklutna Vocational School when Attu children who survived Japanese prison camp were placed there in 1945. Some exaggeration of Japanese "atrocities" against Aleuts, but also some interesting information not found elsewhere.

Conn, Stetson, Engleman, Rose C., and Fairchild, Bryon. Guarding the United States and its Outposts, United States Army in World War II. Washington, D.C.: Office of the Chief of Military History, Dept. of the Army, 1960.

Military campaign in the Aleutians.

Craven, W.F. and Cate, J.L., eds. Plans and Early Operations, January 1939-August 1942. Vol. 4 of The Army Air Forces in World War II. Chicago: University of Chicago Press, 1950.

Gives air actions against Japanese positions on Attu and Kiska during Japanese occupation of the Islands.

Dall, William Healy. "Explorations in the Aleutian Islands and Their Vicinity." American Geographical Society, Journal, 5(1874):243-45.

Discussion of hydrographic, geodetic, and topographic work carried out by U.S. Coast Survey in Aleutians in 1873.

Darling, G.A. "There She Blows!" Alaska Sportsman, 3(May, 1937):13-17, 19-20.

Whaling from Akutan Island whaling station in 1936.

Dawson, George M. "The Extinct Northern Sea-Cow and Early Russian Explorations in the North Pacific." Canadian Field Naturalist, 7(January, 1894):151-61.

Russian discovery of the Aleutian Islands and exploitation of fur resources.

Deane, Leslie. "It's Safe to Go Ahead." Alaska Sportsman 4(August, 1938): 20-23, 28, 30.

Discusses lighthouses in Aleutian Islands and along Alaska coast as aids to navigation.

DeArmond, Robert N. "The Wreck of the James Allen." Alaska Life, 8 (December, 1945):15-18.

Wreck of whaling bark off Amlia Island in 1894.

Denmead, Talbot and Dodd, Esther E. "Whaling on the West Coast of North America, 1911-1938." Sixth Pacific Science Conference, Proceedings, 1939, 3(1940):237-39.

Statistics on numbers, size, sex, and species of whales taken, emphasizing 1937 and 1938 seasons, at Akutan.

Desautels, R.J., McCurdy, A.J., Flynn, J.D. and Ellis, R.R. Archaeological Report, Amchitka Island, Alaska, 1969-70. U.S. Atomic Energy Commission, Division of Technical Information, 1971.

Important survey and testing on Amchitka.

DeVenne, George L. "Blue Gold of the Aleutians." Alaska Sportsman, 5(July, 1939):8-9, 22-24.

Fox ranching in the Aleutians, written by a master of one of the ranching vessels. Good description of trapping activities and techniques on Kanaga, Umnak, Amchitka, and Islands of the Four Mountains.

Driscoll, Joseph. War Discovers Alaska. Philadelphia: J.B. Lippencott Company, 1943.

Journalistic account of invasion of Attu and Kiska, military preparations in Alaska for the invasion of the Islands, and military construction.

Dumond, Don E., Conton, Leslie, and Shields, Harvey M. "Eskimos and Aleuts on the Alaska Peninsula: A Reappraisal of Port Moller Affinities." Arctic Anthropology, 12(No. 1, 1975):9-67.

Difficulty of marking clear boundary between Eskimos and Aleuts on Alaska Peninsula; continuity of material culture in the area.

Duncan, Ray. "The Aleuts Go Home." Yank, May 18, 1945.

Describes the departure of the Aleuts from southeastern Alaska back to their homes after Japanese threat had been removed.

"Facts About the Foggy Aleutians." Science Digest, 12(September, 1942): 90-92.

Physical features, population, and short historical sketch about Aleutians.

Farrelly, Theodore S. "Aleutian Stepping Stones." Yale Review, 32 (December, 1942):280-88.

History of Russian occupation of Aleutians.

Fisher, Edna M. "The Sea Otter, Past and Present." Sixth Pacific Science Congress, Proceedings, 1939, 3(1940);223-36.

History of sea otter trade and hunting activities in Aleutians and along Alaskan coast.

Ford, Corey. Short Cut to Tokyo; the Battle for the Aleutians. New York: Charles Scribner's Sons, 1943.

Story of Japanese attack on Attu and Kiska and preparations for American invasion of Aleutians. Interesting material on Aleuts, as Ford was out in the Aleutians before the war writing magazine articles.

Freiday, Dean. "The Aleutians, Island Necklace of the North." Natural History, 54(December, 1945):444-55.

Photographs of eastern Aleutians. Good topographic description and discussion of volcanic crater on Umnak.

_____. "The Seals and the Sealers." Alaska Life, 8(October, 1945): 30-37.

Pribilof Islands and methods of taking fur seals.

Frenkel, R.E. "Attu, Alaska." U.S. Naval Pacific Range, Report No. 14. Riverside, California: 1960.

Climate, topography, military occupation of Attu.

Garfield, Brian. The Thousand-Mile War; World War II in Alaska and the Aleutians. Garden City, N.Y.: Doubleday & Company, Inc., 1969.

Although journalistic, probably the best account of the Japanese occupation and American recapture of Attu and Kiska. Some mention of Aleuts captured on Attu, and those relocated in Southeast Alaska.

Gilman, William. Our Hidden Front. New York: Reynal and Hitchcock, Inc., 1944.

Journalistic account of invasion of Attu and Kiska. Interesting description of Aleuts.

Golder, Frank A. "Guide to Materials for American History in Russian Archives." Carnegie Institution of Washington, Publication, No. 239. Washington, D.C.: Government Printing Office, 1917.

Golodoff, Innokenty. "The Last Days of Attu Village." As told to Karl W. Kenyon. Alaska Sportsman, 32(December, 1966):8-9.

Golodoff was one of the Attu survivors who spent three years in Japan. Short account, but only one of its kind.

Handleman, Howard. Bridge to Victory; the Story of the Reconquest of the Aleutians. New York: Random House, 1943.

Description of campaign, as well as soldiers' life and living conditions in the Aleutians.

Hatch, F.J. "The Aleutian Campaign." Roundel, 14(No. 4, 1963):18-23.

Royal Canadian Air Force operations in Aleutians, 1942-43.

Hudson, Will E. Icy Hell: Experiences of a Newsreel Cameraman in the Aleutian Islands, Eastern Siberia, and the Arctic Fringe of Alaska. London: Constable & Co., LTD., 1937.

Hinckley, Theodore C. and Hinckley, Caryl. "Ivan Petroff's Journal of a Trip to Alaska in 1878." Journal of the West, 5(January, 1966): 25-70.

Portion of the journal describes Petroff's collecting of historical material in Aleutians. Good discussion of life on the islands in the late nineteenth century.

Hunt, William R. Arctic Passage; the Turbulent History of the Land and People of the Bering Sea, 1697-1975. New York: Charles Scribner's Sons, 1975.

Historical overview of the Bering Sea area, including Aleutian Islands.

Hurt, W.R. "Artifacts from Shemya, Aleutian Islands." American Antiquity, 16 (July, 1950):68-69.

Small collection of artifacts from Near Islands; not enough to place them in Aleut cultural framework.

Hutchinson, H.B. "One way is Through Alaska." United States Naval Institute, Proceedings, 70(January, 1944):1-9.

Strategic location of Aleutians for bringing war to Japanese home islands.

Jones, Ernest Lester. "Report of Alaska Investigations in 1914."
    Washington, D.C.: Government Printing Office, 1915.

    Fisheries investigation of 1914; includes fox farming and full dis-
    cussion of condition and activities of Pribilof Islands natives.

Keithan, Edward L. "Let's Lease an Island." Alaska Sportsman, 7(June,
    1941):14-15, 27-29.

    Some information on Pribilofs and Aleutian Islands.

Kihn, W. Langdon. "Aleut Faces." Natural History, 51(February, 1943):
    72-73.

    Interesting drawings of Aleuts evacuated from Atka during World
    War II.

King, Don. "Edmonton to Kiska; Experiences on the U.S. Air Supply Route
    from Edmonton to Alaska." Canadian Aviation, 18(August, 1945):82, 84.

    Canadian contribution to the war effort in Alaska and the Aleutians.

Kitchener, C.D. "The Fighting 'Earth Movers.'" Alaska Life, 7(July, 1944):
    3-16.

    Military construction in Alaska, including Aleutians, during World
    War II. Some photographs. Discussion of difficulties of construc-
    tion in Aleutian terrain and climate.

Lippold, Lois K. "Mammalian Remains from Aleutian Archaeological Sites:
    A Preliminary Report." Arctic Anthropology, 9(No. 2, 1972):113-15.

    Simultaneous utilization of food resources on Nikolski Bay area is
    seen as basis for cultural stability of Aleuts in the region.

McCartney, Allen P. "An Archaeological Site Survey and Inventory for the
    Alaska Peninsula, Shumagin Islands and Other Islands of the Alaska
    Peninsula, 1973." Unpublished report submitted to the Refuges
    Branch, U.S. Fish and Wildlife Service, Anchorage, Alaska, July, 1973.

    Site locations and descriptions of historic sites on the lower
    Alaska Peninsula and Shumagins. Important source.

_____. "An Archaeological Site Survey and Inventory for the Aleutian
    Islands National Wildlife Refuge, Alaska, 1972." Unpublished report
    submitted to the Wilderness Studies Branch, U.S. Fish and Wildlife
    Serivce, Anchorage, Alaska, November, 1, 1972.

    Site inventory, discussion of history of archaeological research in
    Aleutians.

_____. "Prehistoric Cultural Integration Along the Alaska Peninsula."
    Anthropological Papers of the University of Alaska, 16(no. 1, 1974):
    59-84.

Cultural interaction on Alaska Peninsula as drawn from archaeological investigations at Port Moller and Izembek Lagoon.

Martin, Fredericka. "Pribilof Sealers--Serfs of the North." Institute of Ethnic Affairs, Newsletter, 3(May-June, 1948):1-4.

Effect of decline in wages for Pribilof sealers.

Martin, Paul James. "Our Cinderella Islands." Alaska Life, 11(April, 1948):16-18.

Strategic importance of Aleutian Islands in relation to Asia.

Matthews, Courtland W. Aleutian Interval. Seattle: Frank McCaffrey, Publishers, 1949.

Poetry on Aleutian campaign of 1943, written by American soldier.

Milan, Leda Chase. "Ethnohistory of Disease and Medical Care Among the Aleut." Anthropological Papers of the University of Alaska, 16 (August, 1974):15-40.

Long, interesting, valuable article on significance of disease and medical problems to Aleut culture change. Some of suggestions in conclusion may be doubtful.

Morgan, Lael. "Phasing Out the Aleutians--Again." Alaska, 41(November, 1975):34-39, 78.

Life in Aleutians in the face of decline in salmon fishing.

Morison, Samuel Eliot. Aleutians, Gilberts and Marshalls, June 1942-April 1944. Vol. 7 of History of United States Naval Operations in World War II. Boston: Little, Brown & Co., 1951.

Discussion of American reoccupation of Aleutian Islands.

_____. Coral Sea, Midway, and Submarine Actions, May 1942-August 1942. Vol. 4 of History of United States Naval Operations in World War II. Boston: Little, Brown & Co., 1949.

Japanese attack on Dutch Harbor and invasion of Aleutians within broader framework of war in the Pacific.

Nelson, Willis H. And Barnett, Frank. "A Burial Cave on Kanaga Island, Aleutian Islands." American Antiquity, 20(April, 1955):387-92.

Discusses cultural material gathered from this cave.

Nutchuk /Simeon Oliver7, and Hatch, Alden. Back to the Smoky Sea. New York: Julian Messner Inc., 1946.

Sequel to Son of the Smoky Sea. Discusses World War II in the

Aleutians. Particularly important for reminiscences of Attu before the war, and Attu Aleuts' fear of Japanese.

Paneth, Philip. Alaska, Backdoor to Japan. London: Alliance Press, Ltd., 1943.

General description of Alaska during the war, and strategic position of Aleutian Islands.

Potter, Jean. Alaska Under Arms. New York: Macmillan, 1942.

Journalistic account of Alaska and Aleutians in early years of World War II. Some information on Natives.

Ransom, Jay Ellis. "Life was Simple at Umnak." Alaska Sportsman, 10 (September, 1944):14-15, 26-30.

Life, climate, and Natives of Umnak Island before World War II.

Richardson, Harold W. "Alaska and the Aleutians." In W. Bowman, et. al., Bulldozers Come First; the Story of U.S. War Construction in Foreign Lands. New York: McGraw Hill, 1944.

Problems of military construction in Aleutians.

Russell, Capt. James S. "The Aleutian Campaign." In The Campaigns of the Pacific War, ed. by Rear Admiral R.A. Ofstie. Washington, D.C.: U.S. Strategic Bombing Survey, 1946.

Good information on Aleutian Campaign. Provides lists of composition of Japanese and American forces involved in the Aleutians.

Sekora, Lynda. "A Visit to Kanaga Island." Alaska, 38(November, 1972):23-24.

Visit to abandoned fox farm on Kanaga. Some information on history of fox farming on the island.

Shaneman, R.D. "Service Corps Operations in the Aleutians." Canadian Army Journal, 8(July, 1954):129-31.

Canadian contribution to the war effort in Alaska.

Sarafian, Winston L. "Smallpox Strikes the Aleuts." Alaska Journal, 7(Winter, 1977):48-52.

Brief relation of smallpox epidemic of 1837-38 and its disastrous effects on Aleut population.

Sokol, Anthony E. "Russian Expansion and Exploration in the Pacific." American Slavic and East European Review, 11(April, 1952):85-105.

Thompkins, Stuart Ramsay, "After Bering: Mapping the North Pacific." British Columbia Historical Quarterly, 19(January and April, 1955).

Townshend, Joan B. "Mercantilism and Societal Change: An Ethnohistorical Examination of Some Essential Variables." Ethnohistory, 22(Winter, 1975):21-32.

Importance of fur trade in influencing culture change. Particularly interesting is discussion of the importance of the half-breed creoles in this trade.

Turner, Christy G., II. "Archaeological Reconnaissance of Amchitka Island, Alaska. Arctic Anthropology, 7(no. 2, 1970):118-28.

Limited testing done for Atomic Energy Commission in 1968. Notes importance of more extensive testing for meaningful interpretation of population size in this area of Aleutians.

_____. "Preliminary Report of Archaeological Survey and Test Excavation in the Eastern Aleutian Islands, Alaska." Arctic Anthropology, 9 (No.2, 1972):32-35.

Research on Akutan and Akun Islands.

_____, and Turner, J.A. "Progress Report on Evolutionary Anthropological Study of Akun Strait District, Eastern Aleutians, Alaska, 1970-71." Anthropological Papers of the University of Alaska, 16(No. 1, 1974):27-57.

Akutan Island village site. Akutan is a cultural, marine, and geographic bottleneck, and helped preserve integrity of other Aleutian communities to the west.

Tyler, Charles Marion. Alaska and the Aleutian Islands. San Francisco, 1887.

General description of the area in the 1880s.

U.S. Dept. of the Interior. "The Pribilof Report; Living Conditions Among the Natives of the Pribilof Islands and Other Communities of the Bering Sea." Washington, D.C.: Government Printing Office, 1949.

Government investigation and hearings concerning problems confronting Natives in area after World War II. Good source for this type of information.

U.S. Fish and Wildlife Service. Aleutian Islands Wilderness Study Report. Anchorage: 1973.

Excellent source for general background on Aleutian prehistory, history, and environment. Also has bibliography on environment.

U.S. Library of Congress, Division of Bibliography. "Aleutian Islands; a List of References." Compiled by Grace Hadley Fuller under the direction of Florence S. Hellman. Washington, D.C. Government Printing Office, 1943.

337 entries. Some very obscure information, up through Japanese attack on Aleutians.

U.S. Library of Congress, Law Library, Foreign Law Section. "Russian Administration of Alaska and the Status of Alaska Natives." Washington, D.C.: Government Printing Office, 1950.

Good discussion of the development of Russian imperial control in Alaska. Translations of pertinent Russian documents.

U.S. War Department. The Capture of Attu, as Told by the Men who Fought There. Washington, D.C.: Infantry Journal, 1944.

Compilation of interesting, brief accounts of the battle for Attu Island. Personalized military history.

U.S. War Department, Military Intelligence Division. "Extracts From Diary Found on the Body of a Japanese Officer on the Island of Attu." Explorer's Journal, 22 (Spring, 1944):2-5.

Feelings of Japanese medical officer during last few days of Japanese resistance. Horrifying, pathetic.

Van Gilder, Jack. "The 'Battle' of St. George Island." Alaska Sportsman, 10(October, 1944):14-15, 35-38.

Soldiers' activities on St. George in Pribilofs during World War II.

Wardman, George. A Trip to Alaska; a Narrative of What was Seen and Heard During a Summer Cruise in Alaskan Waters. San Francisco: S. Carson & Co., 1884.

Trip on steamer Rush in 1879. Information on Pribilofs and Aleutian Islands, sealing, and Natives.

Wheaton, Helen. "An Excuse to Visit Atka." Alaska Sportsman, 8(November, 1942):14-15, 18, 20-22.

Story of a Japanese "sealing vessel" which "accidentally" arrived off Atka. Author is sure that Japanese were trying to find out about available harbors in Aleutians. Discusses Natives' fear of Japanese.

Wheaton, T.H. and Wheaton, Helen. "I Trapped Foxes on Kiska." Alaska Sportsman, 10(January, 1944):18-20, 23.

White, Anlis. "A Few Months on Attu." Alaska Sportsman, 13(March, 1947): 14-15, 28-29.

Life of American troops on Attu after Island recaptured from Japanese.

Wolf, Estelle. "The Stepping Stones to Our Back Door." Alaska Sportsman,

9(January, 1943):10-11, 26-28.

Climate, geography, and very short history of Aleutians.

It would probably be of little purpose to give (or try to give) a
description of all archive holdings concerning the Aleutian Islands.
There are too many such holdings that I know about, and probably even
more than I could guess. A good starting point is Robert A. Frederick's
"Caches of Alaskana; Library and Archival Sources of Alaskan History,"
Alaska Review, 2(Fall & Winter, 1966-67):39-79.

Some of the more particular archival sources which I have found for
the Aleutians are as follows:

University of Alaska Archives, Fairbanks
    considerable amount of photographs in the Rhoda Thomas collection;
    microfilm copy of the Pribilof Island logbooks; photographs of World
    War II in the Aleutians; Fredericka Martin collection, which contains
    information on the Pribilofs in 1941-42; many aspects of Aleutian
    history in various collections.

Alaska Historical Library, Juneau
    Samuel Applegate Papers; Applegate was a fur trader and businessman
    of Unalaska. Papers cover period up to 1925.

Syracuse University Library
    Sherrod Papers, 1925-63, including material on World War II in
    Aleutians.

Stanford University Library
    Alaska Commercial Company Papers, 1868-1940.

Columbia University Library
    Theordore S. Farrelly Papers relating to Russian colonization of
    Alaska.

Federal Archives and Records Center, Seattle
    Alaska Native Service Records (Juneau office and Seattle office):
    papers of the Governors of Alaska also have a lot of material on
    Aleutians.

Bancroft Library, University of California, Berkeley Petroff papers;
    translations of Russian sources; photographs, maps, etc. There is
    a guide to the Bancroft collections.

National Archives, Washington
    Numerous record groups containing Aleutian material; a typescript

guide to these is in the University of Alaska archives.

Library of Congress
    Russian Orthodox Church of Alaska records; also Russian-American
    Company records.

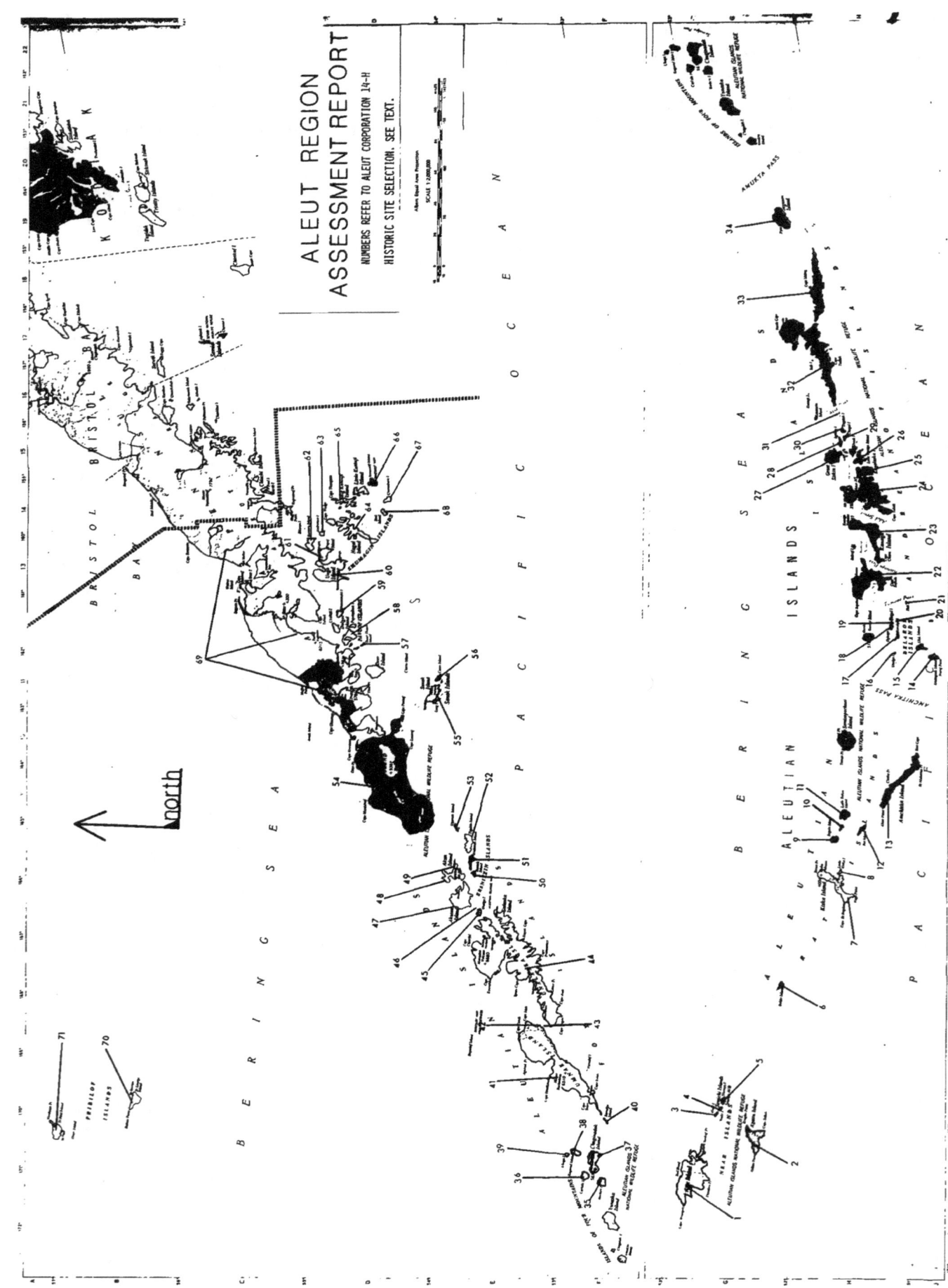

ALEUT REGION
ASSESSMENT REPORT

NUMBERS REFER TO ALEUT CORPORATION 14-H
HISTORIC SITE SELECTION. SEE TEXT.

Albers Equal Area Projection

SCALE 1:2,000,000

north

Island No.	Name	No. of selected 14(h)(1) Sites	File code of selected sites	Unselected sites	File code of unselected sites
1	Attu	25	AU-1 - AU-25		
2	Agattu	10	AG-1 - AG-10		
3	Alaid	1	AI-1		
4	Nizki	4	NZ-1 - NZ-4		
5	Shemya	4	SH-1 - SH-4		
6	Buldir	1	BL-1		
7	Kiska	7	KS-1 - KS-5, KS-7 - KS-8		
8	Little Kiska	1	KS-6		
9	Segula	1	SL-1		
10	Khvostof	1	KH-1		
11	Little Sitkin	3	LS-1 - LS-3		
12	Rat	4	RI-1 - RI-4		
13	Amchitka	78	AC-1 - AC-78		
14	Amatignak	2	AM-1 - AM-2		
15	Ulak	3	UK-1 - UK-3		
16	Unalga	1	UN-1		
17	Kavalga	4	KV-1 - KV-4		
18	Ogliuga	2	OL-1 - OL-2		
19	Skagul	1	SK-1		
20	Tag Islands	1	TI-1		
21	Ilak	2	IL-1 - IL-2		
22	Tanaga	12	TN-1 - TN-12		
23	Kanaga	28	KN-1 - KN-28		
24	Adak	76	AD-1 - AD-76		
25	Kagalaska	5	KA-1 - KA-5		
26	Little Tanaga	2	LT-1 - LT-2		
27	Great Sitkin			1[1]	
28	Igitkin	1	IT-1		
29	Chugul	1	CL-1		
30	Tagalak	1	TK-1		
31	Oglodak	1	OG-1		
32	Atka	18	AT-1 - AT-7, AT-15, AT-19, AT-21 - AT-26, AT-34 - AT-36	19	AT-8 - AT-14, AT-16 - AT-18, AT-20, AT-27 - AT-33, AT-37
33	Amlia	17	AL-3 - AL-19	2	AL-1 - AL-2
34	Seguam	1	SU-1		
35	Herbert	1	HR-1		
36	Carlisle	3	CR-1 - CR-3		
37	Chuginadak	4	CG-1 - CG-4		
38	Kagamil	6	KG-1 - KG-6		
39	Uliaga	2	UL-1 - UL-2		
40	Samalga	1	SM-1	1	SM-2
41	Umnak	6	UM-19 - UM-21, UM-26 - UM-28	29	UM-1 - UM-18, UM-22 - UM-25 UM-29 - UM-35
42	Pustof	1	PI-1		
43	Shiprock	1	SR-1		
44	Unalaska	14	US-1 - US-6, US-15 - US-16, US-19, US-38 - US-39, US-44, US-47 - US-48	36	US-7 - US-14, US-17 - US-18, US-20 - US-37, US-40 - US-43, US-45 - US-46 US-49 - US-50
45	Unalga			1[2]	
46	Baby Islands			1[3]	
47	Akutan			1[4]	
48	Akun	2	AN-9, AN-11	8	AN-1 - AN-8
49	Tanginak	1	AN-10		
50	Rootok			1[5]	
51	Avatanak			1[6]	
52	Tigalda	1	TG-1		
53	Ugamak			1[7]	
54	Unimak	5	UI-5 - UI-9	4	UI-1 - UI-4
55	Sanak			3	SI-1 - SI-3
56	Caton	1	SI-4		
57	Outer Iliasik	1	OI-1		
58	Dolgoi			1	DL-34
59	Wosnesenski	1	WS-33		
60	Unga			4	UG-26, UG-W, UG-X, UG-Y
61	Popof			2	PO-V, PO-24
62	Korovin	1	KR-23	2	KR-3, KR-U
63	Andronica	1	AA-1		
64	Nagai	2	NG-1 - NG-2		
65	Big Koniuji	1	BK-11		
66	Simeonof	6	SF-13 - SF-18		
67	Chernabura	3	CH-19 - CH-21		
68	Bird	1	BD-22		
69	Alaska Peninsula	27	PN-27 - PN-31, PN-36 - PN-39, PN-41 - PN-45, PN-85 - PN-86, PN-90 - PN-97, PN-99, PN-R, PN-T	13	PN-2 - PN-3, PN-32, PN-87 - PN-89, PN-98, PN-S, PN-AA, PN-BB, PN-CC, PN-DD, PN-EE
70 & 71	St. George & St. Paul (Pribilofs)			(?)[8]	
Total		412		131	

[1]Several families were known to have lived on Great Sitkin Island in the eighteenth century, but no specific site location is known; WSR, p. 110.

[2]A nineteenth-century settlement was noted on the south shore of Unalga Island, but no specific location is given; Ibid., p. 104.

[3]A settlement site was reported on "one of the small central islands of the group," but no specific location is given; Ibid.

[4]One specific site location is noted for Akutan Island, but there were probably at least seven villages on the island in the early nineteenth century; Ibid.

[5]A village, abandoned in the mid-nineteenth century, is noted for Rootok Island, but no specific location is given; Ibid.

[6]One village site is noted for Avatanak Island, but no specific location is given; Ibid., p. 103.

[7]A large village on Ugamak Island was noted to have been abandoned in the 1820s. No specific location is given for the site; Ibid.

[8]The Pribilof Islands were discovered by the Russian sailor Gerassim Pribilof in 1786. Bancroft, History of Alaska, pp. 192-93. The Islands do not seem to have had a pre-contact population, although after their discovery Aleuts were brought to the Islands to harvest their fur resources. These Aleuts and their descendants remained on St. George and St. Paul. No 14(h)(1) sites were selected on the Pribilofs, as the entire islands were selected as Native villages under ANCSA. The Alaska Division of Parks lists four historic sites in the Pribilofs: Marunich, on St. Paul, the site of an early settlement; the Russian Orthodox Churches on each of the islands; and the Pribilov fur seal rookeries, which are a National Historic Landmark; State of Alaska, Dept. of Natural Resources, Division of Parks, Alaska's Heritage Resources, Vol. Ii, Iventory, Appendix (Alaska Heritage Resource Survey Index), p.165.